D0988197

Rock the World
with your Online Presence

Your Ticket To A Multi-Platinum Linkedin Profile

Contains special Rock & Roll-inspired "insider" guidance from the world's #1 LinkedIn trainer!

Authors:

Mike O Neil & Lori Ruff

Social Media Pioneers | Classic Rock Aficionados
LinkedIn® Authorities | Keynote Speakers | Expert Trainers

WEB	*www.RockTheWorldBook.com*
BLOG	*www.RockTheWorldBlog.com*
LinkedIn Group	*www.JoinRockTheWorld.com*
Facebook Fan Page	*www.RockTheWorldFan.com*

Find Mike and Lori online:

www.LinkedIn.com/in/MikeOneil	*www.LinkedIn.com/in/LoriRuff*
www.Twitter.com/MikeOneilDenver	*www.Twitter.com/LoriRuff*
www.Facebook.com/MikeOneil	*www.Facebook.com/LoriRuff*

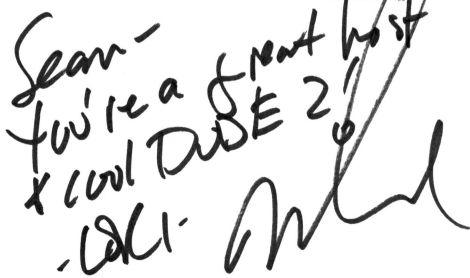

Rock the World Fans

"Mike and I met at a national social media gathering in Boulder, CO. I quickly became aware of how they could help me get LinkedIn to where it was bringing me business. They took my LinkedIn profile from simply existing to full blown rock star status in short order. This book has all the insider information that made me what I am today on LinkedIn. Take a look at what this book can do for you!"

Daisy Whitney, Host of the New Media Minute Internet Television Show
www.daisywhitney.com, www.linkedin.com/in/daisywhitney, @daisywhitney

"This team is a whiz when it comes to getting the most out of your LinkedIn experience. Mike was one of the first individuals I emulated when I got on LinkedIn, and I continue to stay up-to-date with their teachings. Make sure you check out what they have to say!"

Lewis Howes, former Olympic Athlete, Author of the bestselling book LinkedWorking
www.lewishowes.com, www.linkedin.com/lewishowes, @lewishowes

"There are few people that can truly claim to be the 'world-leader' in something. Well Mike O'Neil and Lori Ruff are truly the world leaders when it comes to knowing how to use LinkedIn effectively, and how to train others on using LinkedIn and social media for business success. They are dynamic presenters and trainers. If you want to get ahead in today's globally linked business world, you need this book."

Sam Richter, Top-Selling and Award Winning Author; internationally renowned presenter and Sales Intelligence expert
www.samrichter.com, www.linkedin.com/in/samrichter, @samrichter

"A comprehensive, practical guide with that rare element not often in books . . . fun! They make this book fun to read and fun to implement, and that is very helpful when getting results on LinkedIn, because it's all about paying attention to the details."

Melissa Giovagnoli, Author of Networlding and the upcoming book, 50 Ways to Better Social Networking
www.networlding.com, www.linkedin.com/in/networlding, @networlding

"Mike and Lori show you exactly how to create a rock star LinkedIn profile that's guaranteed to make you an online hit! Get this book to learn how to maximize your online presence now."

Jill Konrath, CEO, Author of Selling to Big Companies
www.SellingtoBigCompanies.com, www.linkedin.com/in/sellingtobigcompanies, *@jillkonrath*

"We repeatedly hired IA to train our association members on LinkedIn. That spawned an address at our national conference in Orlando. The performance was all the rave, the best we had!"

Dan Robitaille, Former President, National Association of Personnel Services (NAPS)
www.xstaff.com, www.linkedin.com/in/danrobitaille

"I was a typical LinkedIn user before I met this team. I had a "complete profile" and got nothing out of it. After taking the IA LinkedIn training and implementing what they recommended, I realized the benefits of a well-developed presence on LinkedIn. This book takes that training to a whole new level."

Viveka von Rosen, Social Media Authority and Women's networking expert
www.alwaysextraordinary.com, www.linkedin.com/in/linkedinexpert, *@linkedinexpert*

"No one has greater depth of knowledge concerning LinkedIn than the team at IA. While LinkedIn may seem straightforward, there is an art and science in utilizing it to its full potential. This book lays the foundation to maximize the ROI using LinkedIn. Well done! I would recommend this book for everyone!"

Jay Deragon, Social Media Authority
www.relationship-economy.com, www.linkedin.com/in/jayderagon, *@jderagon*

"To truly maximize the power of the LinkedIn platform, you need guidance from both a leader and group that uses the tools and trains business owners to create profitable business relationships. Mike O'Neil and Lori Ruff are the leaders and IA is the group. I was totally unaware of the power of LinkedIn as a business platform until I had a session with them. To maximize your time and derive maximum ROI with LinkedIn, buy and use this book. Then watch your business networking rise to new levels!"

David Bullock, Social Media Author and internationally-recognized Social media Expert
www.davidbullock.net, www.linkedin.com/in/davidsbullock, *@davidbullock*

Table of Contents

People who inspired me and helped me get here

This book, this company, this career would not have been possible without some very special help. Certain people were instrumental all along the way. Some inspired me at key moments, while others helped me make strategic decisions in my life that brought me to this point. Writing this book combines two of my passions in life – Social media (LinkedIn in particular) and Rock & Roll music.

It starts with the O'Neil family itself – **Bernie** (Dad), **Nancy** (Mom) and **Barb** (my sister). There were many times that I needed a little (or a lot of) support, and they have always been there for me. If not for them, I might not have even gone to college, being the muscle car guy that I was.

My "mini-me" son **Brendan William O'Neil** also will have some decisions to make when he grows up past his 11 years of age – selecting the blue pill

(what I *should* do with my life) vs. the red pill (what I *want* to do with my life). I chose the blue pull with subtle help of my family.

Getting my post-college career started were **Jack Huber** and **Ed Lewis** of Ramada Corporate HQ. Out of 200 candidates, all more experienced than I, they selected me as the Ramada Corporate "PC Guru." It was my job to try every new PC thing invented to see how we might use it at Ramada. I trained users on how to "format floppies" and a lot more. The license plate on my '78 Firebird Formula read "MR PC".

It was top sales trainer **Tom Hopkins** who inspired me to get out of IT and into computer-networking sales in the 80's, where

I really found my calling. The thing that meant the most – "We get what we want in sales by helping others get what they want".

Next was **Tom Kieffer**, CEO of Connect Computer in Minnesota, who really taught me the power of bringing it all together: hardware, software, support, and training. I sold a lot of Microsoft LAN Manager software and training to 3M and had Rollerblade as a client... still have an original pair of "Roller-blade Macroblades".

When I started my own business in 2003 (so as not to look unemployed), it was **Herm Braun** helped me get Integrated Alliances going: great company name. We were fellow engineers throwing networking parties and designing wireless networks.

It was my ex-wife, **Diane O'Neil**, who first got me thinking about writing a book. She wrote some amazing books about technology for children. At the time, the subject just had not yet come to me.

I learned tricks about producing great networking events (e.g., IA's Social-Net and LinkedIn Live events) from experts **Sheila Martin**, **Donna Feldman** and **Maita Lester** (who runs the Rockies Venture Club). Maita joined LinkedIn in 2004 and just recently started getting serious about it. She deserves and receives special 1-on-1 training from me.

I am grateful to Sabrina Risely of Behind the Moon, for taking over our popular SocialNet networking events in Denver. As our business model changed and more frequent travel made monthly events difficult to produce, Sabrina grew her local networking business model to a point where the hand-off was a natural decision. I know our friends and fans are in good hands with her.

It was a wintry morning at Starbucks in 2006 somewhere in the Denver Tech Center with friend and business-capital expert **Kevin Johansen** that the LinkedIn training idea germinated. I don't drink coffee so I brought a Moun-tain Dew (maybe two) with me and Kevin was sportin' the 'Jo'.

Spending time with LinkedIn founder **Reid Hoffman** is something that I probably didn't fully appreciate at the time. I was his "handler" at the Rockies Venture Club Angel Capital Summit.

It was the success of **Jason Alba**'s book titled *I'm on LinkedIn, Now What?* that proved there was a market for social media books and inspired me to complete this 2 year project. Jason's book sales remain strong and for very good reasons.

Lifetime friend **Paul Breckner** has always believed in me, and in Integrated Alliances as well. He generously funded 1) the growth that took us national, and 2) getting this book to market.

I have met and developed professional relationships through social media, through speaking and training, through networking, and through traveling. People like **Patrick O'Malley**, a fellow funny Irishman and LinkedIn speaker/ trainer based in Boston. There are so many...

My early mentor, **Scott Allen**, will remember when I picked him up at the airport and we ran out of gas on the way to his hotel. He had his laptop and wireless broadband card out and fired up when I returned from the gas station, container in hand. That night I assembled my Denver LinkedIn posse for a night of drinks with Scott.

A recent mentor is **Joel Comm**, author of Twitter Power, who is a Social media expert and inventor of the iFart application for the iPhone. Joel is a master at commanding a crowd and creating a highly engaged audience. His attention to proven strategies mirrors many of our own methodologies here at IA.

When getting the Integrated Alliances social media business up and going, it was **Dave Taylor** that gave me direction. Dave taught the very first LinkedIn trainings we did in early 2006. Dave returns to write the forward in this book. That's fitting since he is also a true rock & roll aficionado.

Paul Coughlin helped develop IA's national-expansion strategy. He has stepped in at many points along the way to help us with our newest and highest tech systems, always providing valuable honest advice as only a friend will do.

I consider **Marc Freedman** of Dallas Blue to be my first true peer in this networking and LinkedIn business. We both understand the value of events, training and entertainment. Simultaneously and independently, coined the term "LinkedIn Live" for our events. Great minds think alike!

Stan Relihan of Sydney, Australia, put me on the air in the early days of podcasts. All in all, his Connections Show interviewed over 60 of the world's most influential social media personalities, including **Vincent Wright**, **Patrick Crane** (of LinkedIn), **Scott Allen**, **Marc Freedman** (of Dallas Blue), **Christian Mayaud**, **Vint Cerf** (founder of the Internet), **Thomas Power** (of Ecademy), **Dave Mendoza**, **Ron Bates** (#1 on LinkedIn), **Jason Alba**, **Craig Elias**, **Cameron Reilly**, **Melissa Giovagnali** (of Networlding), **Rob McNealey** and **Steven Burda** and me. I was interview #11, speaking on hosting a successful business networking event, a show that was consistently the No. 2 weekly download.

Friends and industry heavyweights **Jay Deragon** and **David Bullock** are driving IA's current thinking in terms of executive engagement in Social media. I am proud of our corporate-level capabilities with this amazing pair and with other like-minded partners.

Dan Robitaille deserves loads of credit for exposing me to the recruiting community, LinkedIn's #1 population. Dan has funded the first 2 recruiting workshops we did, and they spawned 2 of our best offerings - LinkedIn for Recruiting and LinkedIn Network Building.

Jeff Kay deserves special mention for first putting me in front of the camera to deliver training for his eclectic audience of recruiting partners and customers. Our DVD series was a turning point in my career, encouraging me to spend more time in front of live audiences and in front of the camera.

Ray Hutchins acting both alone and on behalf of the TiE-Rockies association gave me lots of unselfish, super-timely help along the way. He introduced me to some of the most amazing mentors ever, and helped us launch our duo-speaker training format.

Special thanks go out to the many IA volunteers and helpers who stepped up to the plate when there was a need or an opportunity – always answering the call and moving right up into roles that needed filling.

Dave Westfall came in and lit up the national expansion, produced amazing Integrated Alliances holiday parties, and brought IA up on some very sophisticated software systems.

Lyndle Savage Sr was a regular attendee of our classes. As IA grew, he came on board to head up business development. He worked tirelessly and pitched in with training development, instructing classes, hosting the LinkedIn Live Lounge, and more to help propel our success.

Taking Integrated Alliances to its current level is **Lori Ruff** who joined the IA executive team at a very interesting time. Under Lori, IA grew its training offerings from a few to over 10. Lori created IA's professional services practice and manages it still. She is the driving force behind my vision.

David Reingold, Ed Riefenstahl and **Valerie Riefenstahl** saw the Integrated Alliances vision early on, they helped transform the Integrated Alliances LinkedIn training business concept from a little company in Denver, Colorado, into the world's first national social media training organization.

Bob Smith jumped in to assist with the strategic reins of Integrated Alliances, placing it on this path to "controlled hyper growth."

Lori Ruff and I appear together on stage, in trainings, and even on Webinars. Our energy, personalities, and depth of knowledge are amazing to see. Presentations are always new and a bit spontaneous.

The Roadmap to this Book

Very special thanks go out to the following special friends and partners who helped get this book done and off to market...

- To **Lori Ruff** for everything one could imagine including research, writing, editing, testing, and training and development expertise. At the moment we were set to go the printer, she got access to the new user interface and spent four solid days and nights to pour through the book yet again so we could bring you the latest information and major breaking news.

- To **Viveka von Rosen, April Stensgard, Diana Gats, Lucinda Ruch** and **Deborah Smith** for their proofreading and content advice.

- To **Melissa Giovagnoli** of Networlding Publishing for getting the entire book project moving and completed.

- To **Bob Todd** for his incredibly creative work on screen shots and cover design. He's the TRUE Andy Warhol fan.

- To **JD Gershbein** for his LinkedIn expertise and his brilliant and humorous cartoons.

- To **Andrew Curtis** of FUEL VM for the spot-on, MTV-style interior book design.

- To **John Malysiak** for initial editing and especially to **Michael J Dowling** for the amazing professional editing of this "not so normal" book.

- To **Neil McKenzie** for his amazing photography, including the now famous shot on the cover of the book.

- To **Tom McWhirter, Mark Steele** and **Charlie Snyder, Daniel V Buckley, Jeremy Rowan** for development of the videos and DVDs that accompany this book, and to **Sara Francis** of **Photomirage** for the incredible book trailer.

- To **Dave Taylor** for his early inspiration on our LinkedIn trainings and for his insightful Rock & Roll-inspired introduction.

- To **Miles Austin** for strategy and business advice on the original book work.

- To **Lewis Howes** for his support and acknowledgement of me as an inspiration in his great LinkedIn book – LinkedWorking.

- To **Joel Comm** for showing us how the book and a speaking career can be combined to help others while simultaneously helping ourselves.

- To **Bob Smith** for leadership, vision and business expertise that allowed us to be creative and concentrate on public speaking, writing, and training development.

- And especially to **Paul Breckner**, CEO of Data Sales, Inc., for his generous support of this book project and his long-time friendship.

Introduction

I'm a baby boomer, just like Mike O'Neil, so when I saw the Rolling Stone / Andy Warhol-inspired cover art, I knew we were in sync on what we thought about becoming successful in the world of social media and, specifically, LinkedIn. As I read through this book, though, I realized that not only do we both think in terms of music, we listen to the same bands!

As I write this introduction, I'm listening to Bruce Springsteen singing about the "Empty Sky" from his album *The Rising*. By the time I finish writing, I will have listened to Donald Fagan, Al Jarreau, Kate Bush, Sting, James Taylor, The Beatles and the Alan Parsons Project.

I think it's a Zen thing, actually: Listen to the lyrics of the songs on your playlist and you'll realize that they're talking about what's going on in your life. Mike understands, and that's why the theme of this LinkedIn mastery guide is rock 'n roll music. And, yes, you do want to become a LinkedIn rock star!

The modern world has become far more connected than we'd ever have realized even twenty years ago (I used to work at HP's R&D laboratory, so I was supposed to be able to predict the future.) We're now hyper-connected, and while the size of my network doesn't approach Mike's, I now have over a thousand connections on Facebook and just about the same number of LinkedIn connections. On LinkedIn, that's enough to link me to 14,081,000+ professionals, according to the site.

Does it matter? Are these really 14 million or, heck, a thousand of my best friends? No, of course not. But as you'll learn from reading this book, it's not about digital pals replacing your real-life friends; it's about extending and expanding your professional network (and personal network) to enable you to make connections in companies and industries you care about, to find hiring managers, or, flipping that coin, to find highly qualified candidates.

That's the beauty of LinkedIn. Because success in the future isn't about whom you know, but rather who they know, and so on. You might only have a circle of seventy connections on LinkedIn, but if each of them has a few hundred connections, it leaps extraordinarily quickly into the tens of thousands of people that you can communicate with directly, people whose resumes and professional credentials are there for you to peruse.

And, like being a star on the basketball team at school, you can't just rely on the skills and expertise of your teammates to win the game: you have to put in the proverbial 110 percent, to be a great, enthusiastic player too. In the digital world, it means you have to ask yourself "What can I give back?" and "How can I help you?"

My personal philosophy perhaps sums it up nicely: Always give more than you want to get back. If someone asks you to connect them to another person, do so gracefully. Be honest, but be forthcoming and helpful. It'll pay off in spades.

The Beatles put it thusly:

"And in the end, the love you take is equal to the love you make." (The Beatles, "The End," from the brilliant album *Abbey Road*)

But I won't end with a Beatles quote. Instead, let's try this one:

"Look for me out there, someday I'll touch the blue, blue sky."
Alan Parsons Project, "Blue Blue Sky,"
from the album On Air.

Rock on!

- Dave Taylor
http://www.linkedin.com/in/DaveTaylor
http://www.DaveTaylorOnline.com/
Twitter: @DaveTaylor

The Connection between Rock Music and Popular Social Media Platforms like LinkedIn

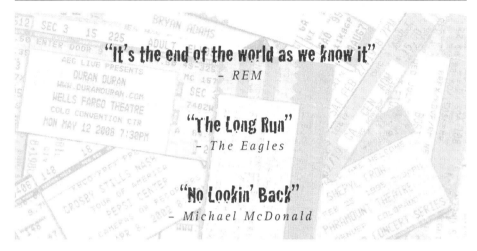

"It's the end of the world as we know it"
- *REM*

"The Long Run"
- *The Eagles*

"No Lookin' Back"
- *Michael McDonald*

Just as the Internet changed everything when it came around in the 90s, Social media is changing everything in this century. It really is "the end of the world as we know it," especially in how relationships, both social and business, are being formed.

- Recruiters are using online tools like LinkedIn to find and recruit candidates. It is the end of mailing in resumes, searching Monster.com, etc.

- Sales professionals are hooked on the inside information they glean from LinkedIn. It is the end of blind cold calls, purchasing lists, etc.

- Business-development professionals have entirely new doors open to them to find and nurture business partners that formerly happened only through "inside connections" or by chance. They now use LinkedIn to find, contact and engage new business partners that they would have never known about.

In "the long run," this will be a standard way of doing business. Well, the long run is getting shorter, isn't it? Were the Eagles onto something?

Just like a CD can now be cut in a week, using hundreds of dollars worth of equipment and a basement, a business team can be formed in short order and with little investment. Lists of prospects can be assembled and contacted in little time as well.

There is really "No Lookin' Back." The speed of business is accelerating, not slowing down, and social media has much to do with it. The culture around social media, with each platform being a bit unique, is stealing the hearts and minds of more and more people – millions more each week.

Back to the music...

There is a real culture around music, and around classic Rock in particular. As you look back at specific points in your life, music from the era inevitably comes to mind. You hear that Boston or Doobie Brothers song on the radio, and it stirs memories of a time, a culture, a special something that you experienced.

It just isn't the same nowadays with the charts being topped by the likes of Jay-Z, Beyoncé, Britney Spears, The Black Eyed Peas, and The Jonas Brothers. Guitar solos are replaced by a slew of scantily clad dancers strutting their stuff in perfect sync to recorded tracks, while musicians wave around their instruments for the cameras.

So, what do we spend our time doing INSTEAD of listening to Casey Kasem's Top 40 show like we did when we were young?

We're listening to classic rock on the radio or on our iPods, and we are on our computers visiting social media sites. For many, that means LinkedIn, Facebook, Twitter, and others that are filled with other people in their 30s, 40s, 50s, and even 60s and 70s!

Social media is such a cultural phenomenon! Many years from now, we will recall it in much the same way as we look back at the Rock & Roll years. We will have relationships that started online firmly established in our lives. We will look back and realize just how the most important relationships in our lives were started and Social media will be a central theme, much like a soundtrack to a really great movie.

It all starts with a profile and – in this comprehensive book – it begins with mastering the LinkedIn Profile. Use this book not only to create your profile, but keep it as a bible anytime you update or tweak your profile. It truly is a great resource for beginning or seasoned users.

Before you get started, here are a few helpful hints:

1. Join **Rock the World** group on LinkedIn and request to join the Integrated Alliances University subgroup (more about groups in Appendix B). Visit **www.JoinRockTheWorld.com** to get started.

2. Take a quick peek at the Appendices; there are resources listed that you will want to access as you take this journey.

3. Additional resources, videos, worksheets and updates can be found online at **www.RockTheWorldBook.com/Extras**. Be sure to visit often for the latest information.

4. Download the Profile Worksheet found at **www.RockTheWorldBook. com/Extras** and use this to record your notes and to maintain your profile. You will be working in this file for much of the next few weeks as you work through this material.

Utilize these resources; follow these simple steps. You will be quite glad you did!

Before we get started

"Start me up"
– The Rolling Stones

This guide will "start you up" in much the same way that Mick Jagger starts you up on stage. It is a rocket ship to establishing your online presence on LinkedIn, so hold on tight. In short order, you will be rocking and rolling on LinkedIn like the true rock star that is lurking within you!

There is a natural fit between the LinkedIn business-social-network platform and business professionals. This is a **play-by-play guide** for success in your professional efforts—whether personally or on behalf of your employer.

This book takes you from just being "on" LinkedIn to being a well-represented user. It helps you build your credibility and online reputation. The return on investment in terms of money and time spent with LinkedIn is the focus of this book because it is the focus of users already online and on LinkedIn.

Third party statistics by @plan (Summer 2008), a company tracking social media statistics, indicate that over 49 percent of individuals on the LinkedIn community are decision-makers. That is a driving force behind the adoption of LinkedIn by sales and marketing professionals. But they are not the only adopters of this powerful platform.

Many of the top and most active people on LinkedIn are recruiters. In addition to finding resources for booking orders, they are actively and/or passively seeking candidates. For that reason and because the fact that LinkedIn profiles seem very similar to a resume, this tool is being adopted by many job seekers. With the addition of more job seekers and professionals in career transition, more and more recruiters turn to LinkedIn as a resource to find the perfect candidate.

As candidates find employment, many continue their participation now focused on applications in business. This further fuels the growth in both numbers of users and regular activity. There are many other professionals who are on the platform and focused because of the power of relationships, keyword searching, LinkedIn groups, Google indexing, and other helpful tools and features.

LinkedIn not only helps you *find* and *communicate* with decision makers, it helps you *form* and *nurture relationships* with them. That can lead to long-lasting and deep business relationships. This helps reduce competition, increase margins, and bring additional opportunities to the table. People on LinkedIn are there to help others on LinkedIn; many just don't know how to get started. That is the reason for this book.

Part of the power of LinkedIn is in how it enables professionals to become a better resource to HELP THEIR CUSTOMERS BE MORE SUCCESSFUL. By mastering the LinkedIn Profile, you start to become a resource to your customers, solidifying relationships that you have with them. One of the most resonating statements ever made by Tom Hopkins, the famous sales trainer, is that as "professionals, we get what we want in life by helping others get what they want in life." LinkedIn greatly enables this time-proven principle.

So, "Let's Go!" (The Cars, 1977)

How to use this book as a guide
– the roadmap

"Show me the way"
– *Peter Frampton*

"Helter Skelter"
– *The Beatles*

This guide is a "show me the way" system to establishing your online presence with LinkedIn, using an easy-to-follow, step-by-step process. After delivering hundreds of LinkedIn training sessions to companies, groups and associations, the process covered in this book is proven time and again to be the most effective.

For the best results, don't go all "Helter Skelter." Follow the order presented here for your first draft and THEN drill down and optimize the sections as you see fit. After all, the guitar solo is never at the beginning of the song, and the encore is always at the end, isn't it?

This book is designed to be a reference that you come back to often. As you develop each area of your LinkedIn profile and adjust your account settings, you prepare for the next step. Do not try to do too much at once. There is no point in getting overwhelmed and giving up before you give yourself a good chance at success! Focus your time, do a little bit each day, and soon you will have perfected your online reputation using LinkedIn.

We provide an overview, followed by a step-by-step process, to get you started on LinkedIn, or to perfecting your LinkedIn profile if you have been on awhile. It really helps to get a 10,000-foot view before you land on the ground so you know what to expect and what the purpose is of all of this stuff.

We know your time is valuable and limited, so we do our best to indicate what is important and what is not worth your time. This will help you focus your energies and get the best possible results.

Generally, the best process is:

1. Gather information for inclusion in your LinkedIn Profile.

2. Combine it into the format presented in this book.

3. Have some others (that may be more experienced on LinkedIn) review your work and make comments on what you might have missed or what might be improved.

4. Use the principles: invite a few people to get used to the process, starting with a few of your friends that are already on LinkedIn. Experience with the search functions will help you write a better LinkedIn Profile. So, go back and give your Profile another look after you have gained some searching experience.

5. Look at the strategies in each of the areas presented and begin implementing one at a time those you wish to use.

 Throughout the book you will find TIPs. These are a sprinkling of best practices and strategies that will reduce your time involvement and increase your effectiveness. These methodologies have been developed by our team of experts over the past four years of training and consulting. Several of our team members have been involved in Internet and professional coaching and training for over ten years. Integrated Alliances is truly a thought leader and a respected and trusted authority, even by many of today's newest experts.

When crafting verbiage for use in your LinkedIn profile, we suggest that you make extensive use of your word processor. Why?

1. The LinkedIn system currently has no spell check capability, and spelling errors only hurt your credibility, just as in a resume or a cover letter.

2. LinkedIn often provides very small windows for you to enter text. In many cases, you can only see a small portion of what you have entered and this in no way resembles how it will look to the user when you save your work.

3. It is good to have an offline backup in case you make a mistake and have to start over, or if you want to use the same language on another platform (such as FastPitch, Facebook, Ecademy or others.)

4. There are additional formatting options in a word processor that are not supported by LinkedIn. You can create all that you like in Word, but the copy/paste process will strip out much of your lovely formatting work.

 Do not use outline formatting. It will insert odd-looking boxes in your profile. If you want to indent, it is better to just enter a special symbol and a few spaces in front of the paragraph.

Create one single file that has each section of text separated by the title of the corresponding section (i.e., Summary, Specialties, Experience). Or put each section on its own page. With your profile completed in your word processor, use the Windows Copy and Paste functions to transfer the text to the appropriate section on LinkedIn. This will make more sense once you start, but trust me here... it is worth the effort!

Consider using Firefox or its cousin, Flock, as your browser. Both have basic Spell Check capabilities built right in. Flock is a real interesting animal in that it has a tremendous number of social media features built-in. Most are integrations with social media platforms OTHER than LinkedIn, but there is always hope that LinkedIn will begin singing from the same sheet of music as its peers for the good of the user community.

Provisions for the trip – a checklist

In order to take this journey, you want to pack what you can to help you along the way. To assist with the "data collection" part of creating your profile, here is a checklist of things you should gather (in no particular order of importance).

- A resume or biography

- A portfolio

- A decent headshot – a photograph of up to 4MB becomes an 80x80 pixel of your smiling face!

- Your blog or articles you have written (If they are online, gather the links as well.)

- Profile language from other social networking sites

- Letters of recommendation

- Information about previous employers, including Websites and marketing materials

- Job titles, descriptions, and start/stop dates (just including the years of your employment is usually fine)

- Significant volunteer experiences, including roles, responsibilities and start/stop dates

- Website addresses you want to include (up to three sites or the URLs for three pages)

- Honors and awards; professional certifications

- An inventory of groups and associations you belong to, that are related to your industry, or related to the industries of your clients and vendors

- An inventory of your professional and personal interests (Include community service interests and things that let people know you live a balanced life!)

- Your contact information that you want to share ... how and why people should contact you.

- Your educational experience: when, where, activities, and societies including higher education and continuing education (i.e., Dale Carnegie or Integrated Alliances University)

- Recommendations from people from your current and previous circles of influence ... both professional and educational (Ask for them if you don't already have them.)

The very first step – signing up

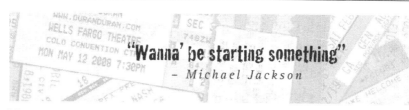

"Wanna' be starting something"
– Michael Jackson

You can't get started in the LinkedIn world until you have a LinkedIn profile, an identity. While LinkedIn makes getting started very easy, getting a sparkling LinkedIn profile takes time and/or some help. So the process is two-fold: "You wanna' be starting something" to get going, and then you can go back and keep refining that something until it is worthy of an encore.

To work with LinkedIn, you must first join and become a member. It is really quite easy to sign up on LinkedIn. You simply type **www.linkedin.com** into your browser. You will arrive at the LinkedIn welcome screen and be asked if you are already a LinkedIn user.

If you are an existing user, this will be very familiar to you. In many cases you will whiz straight on through to the LinkedIn home page bypassing this sign-in screen altogether. LinkedIn, like many programs, can remember that you were there already and will often let you bypass the sign-in screen.

If you are indeed NEW to LinkedIn, you will not go right into LinkedIn. You will need to sign up, and this means that you will be prompted to enter some basic information about yourself starting with your First and Last Name, Email Address and Password. LinkedIn will walk you through some basic steps to get started. It only takes about five minutes to complete these initial steps. Once you have an account started and a foot in the door, it is time to start to really make use of this guide.

The following are two screen shots to illustrate how easy it is to get started:

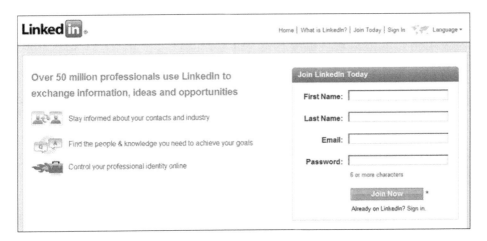

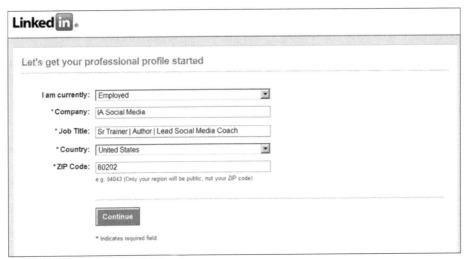

The Amazing LinkedIn User Community – why you are here

"My Hometown"
– Bruce Springsteen

When LinkedIn users are put in a room with one another, they feel an instant connection with one another for a number of reasons. Demographics are one of those reasons. I have personally hosted more than 300 networking events over the years, and I can attest to this. So can the tens of thousands of people who have attended business networking events. Take a look at official LinkedIn demographics and see if you can say that they might be from "My Hometown."

This community is highly concentrated with high level, important people. They are executives, business owners, financiers, recruiters, HR professionals, technologists, sales and marketing professionals, coaches and consultants and much more. As of October 2009, LinkedIn's AVERAGE user demographics (technically "psychographics") are listed as having 15 years of business experience, and being 41 years of age with a six-figure household income.

While LinkedIn began in the San Francisco Bay area, it quickly spread to other large cities around the United States and around the world. The heaviest pockets of users are in the Northeast U.S. (New York, Boston, etc.), the UK, the Netherlands and India. The large-scale spread of LinkedIn users to tier 2 and tier 3 markets around the U.S. is well underway. You can now find large user communities in cities ranging from Seattle to Kansas City, Austin to Miami and in every other city that has a robust business community, as well as many smaller communities where there is a good concentration of professionals who desire a presence on the web.

Because LinkedIn is a web-based community, even individuals in a very small town can be fully engaged with other members of their profession, just as with the Internet in general. It is truly a powerful networking and connection tool.

Contacts vs. Connections – there are major differences

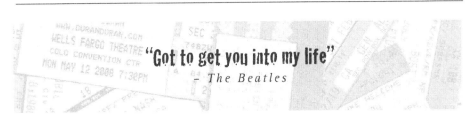

"Got to get you into my life"
– *The Beatles*

The difference between a friend and a stranger is often that you just haven't met the stranger yet. Strangers are not "in your life" yet. Let's face it, we are all born naked, our best friends were strangers at one time. The same goes for our spouses! Just because we don't know someone doesn't mean that they don't have value, or that they might not become important.

The idea behind LinkedIn is the power and benefit one can get from connecting with others. There may be people that YOUR contacts know who can benefit you, and vice versa. Taking that a step farther, there may be people that THEIR contacts know that may benefit you, contacts that they have and so on. LinkedIn actually goes three levels deep in terms of this friend of a friend system of connecting people. At one time, LinkedIn actually went four levels deep. There was no reason given for the elimination of the fourth level, but considering the exponential difference between x3 and x4 times, the software calculations required may have been the culprit. This is complex stuff!

These connections should be viewed as **resources** that can be a benefit to both parties in the LinkedIn system. These resources help to:

- Discover new customers and business partners,

- Receive valuable information that others may have to share,

- Find people with specific skills, experiences, or background,

- Locate people for projects,

- Find people to fill a job opening,

- Find a job or project work,

- Find funding for a business,

- Meet people with similar interests who can prove beneficial to your professional career, or

- Open opportunities for your professional wish list... think about the possibilities if you only "knew someone who..."

LinkedIn Connections are the foundation of all of this activity. To connect with others, you must first have a LINKEDIN PROFILE. The better your LinkedIn profile, the more successful you will be in connecting with others, having your invitation accepted, and realizing the benefits of those relationships.

Your Online Identity – it all starts with a profile

People are only going to get to know you by what you tell them. For the most part, you can say what you like and the "garbage in, garbage out" principle definitely applies. You are in control of what people see and what they know about you. Keep in mind that this is a peer-reviewed network. People who know you well will be reading your profile. Show yourself in as good of a light as possible, but keep it real.

You will constantly improve your LinkedIn profile as you find better ways to describe yourself, what you can do for others, and what works and does not work in terms of bringing in the right kind of opportunities.

Let people get to know the business side of you first and foremost on LinkedIn. The personal side is secondary. This is very different from other social media platforms like Facebook. But there is stil plenty of room for individuality, especially as more and more people similar to you join LinkedIn.

Once you sign up, you are ready to roll up your sleeves and start to "Control your Professional Identity Online."[1] On your personal LinkedIn Home Page you will find a button called **Profile**. It is right at the top. You can select from the **Edit Your Profile** or **View Your Profile** tabs.

This is where you start to craft your LinkedIn profile. Build (edit) your LinkedIn profile one section at a time. The LinkedIn profile is comprised of a number of sections and sub-sections. Some are more important than oth-

---

[1] *http://www.linkedin.com*

ers. In the following pages, we will show you the best methodologies for each section, getting into some very fine details along the way. These details are strategic. They open the door for you to get the maximum benefit from LinkedIn. Like most things in life, what you see first is generally the most important. LinkedIn Profiles are no exception.

So, what exactly is a Profile?

"Who are you?"
- The Who

Your LinkedIn profile is all about "who you are" as a business person. It is a compilation of a lot of business-related information and a few personal things that combine to paint a three-dimensional picture of what you are like to do business with. It is up to you to show people who view your profile the real you; it is up to you to let them know what makes you special.

A very good LinkedIn profile is like a live album, whereas an average LinkedIn profile is more like a studio album (and not a great studio album at that). Which one paints a bigger and better picture of the band?

A LinkedIn profile is your identity on LinkedIn. Where a company's online presence is a Website, an individual has a LinkedIn profile, a detailed record on the LinkedIn website. Some have called it an online resume. This is an oversimplification. Put forward by people who do not understand LinkedIn, but it is not entirely out of the ballpark. Your LinkedIn profile gives you the ability to "Control Your Online Reputation."[2]

[2] *Lori Ruff, Integrated Alliances*

A LinkedIn profile should not be thought of as an online resume. That market is served (quite effectively) by **Monster.com, CareerBuilder.com, HotJobs.com, JibberJobber.com** and many others. People who use those services are predominantly job seekers and recruiters – the jobseekers typically are not currently employed. Although there are many recruiters and job seekers successfully using LinkedIn, for the most part, users are gainfully employed. This is a tool they use IN their business FOR their business.

Think of it this way – your LinkedIn profile is there to help you in two ways: to find and to be found on LinkedIn. People do not get involved on LinkedIn to HIDE. They are, for the most part, there to be FOUND – found by people they WANT to be found by.

Think of a properly formulated LinkedIn profile as a combination of the following:

Your Online Professional Biography

This is a mini website all about you. A bio is all about why you are significant, important, and/or qualified to do what you do. It lists your accomplishments. So it is in a LinkedIn profile.

Your Resume

Your LinkedIn profile indeed has information about work history, skills and education, as well as a summary. However, it is much more robust than what is acceptable on a resume. Experience should be forward-thinking and focused on how your past is relevant to what you do now.

Your Personal Web Page

Your LinkedIn profile has information about your business that is often found on a web page. In fact, LinkedIn even allows you to insert links directly to your web page (up to three actually).

Your Online Advertisement

Your LinkedIn profile tells people what you can do for them: your skills, your capabilities, your offerings. It tells them why you are in the space, what you need, and what you have to offer.

Your Future

Where a resume looks 90 percent back and maybe ten percent forward, your LinkedIn profile is more of a forward-looking document. It tells people what you want to do going forward based on what you have done in the past. This is especially true for the Summary section of your LinkedIn profile.

Your Interests

People like to see more about a person than the 100 percent business side. They like to know more about you, the person. LinkedIn makes it easy to do this, and it even has some very useful tools for you to find others with the same interests. Don't overlook the power of Interests when developing your LinkedIn profile. People do business with people they know and trust. This is where you have a real opportunity to connect to people with whom you have common interests. Even if they do not need your services at the moment, they might open doors to help connect you to people who do!

What a LinkedIn Profile is NOT

It is NOT your picture(s), your favorite songs, your friends, or insignificant information about you. It is a business and not a social tool. MySpace, Facebook and other sites do a very good job in those more social areas.

Purpose of the LinkedIn Profile

Your LinkedIn profile serves many purposes, but the biggest are to help you to be found, to find resources, and to give you credibility in professional circles. Again, people do not use LinkedIn to hide. They are on LinkedIn, for the most part, to be found – found by people they WANT to be found by, and to have a strong footing in which to begin an engagement with others.

Everything in your LinkedIn profile should be written and focused using an "attraction strategy." Design your profile to attract a specific type of audience that is, in general, your target audience. Various professionals write their LinkedIn profiles differently: an executive, a scientist, a telecom sales person or a recruiter will each write with a different focus, a different attraction strategy.

Keep in mind that your profile is not static; once you write it you will want to check it periodically to keep it fresh and relevant to maximize your personal brand.

 Tip! *If you are making regular changes to your profile, you may want to log into your accounts and settings to turn off the "Profile Updates" feature until you are done with the majority of edits. More information can be found in the "Account and Settings" section under "Privacy Settings: Profile and Status Updates."*

The Profile Development Process – a one, and a two and a three and GO

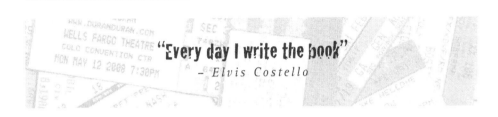

"Every day I write the book"
– *Elvis Costello*

Your LinkedIn profile is like a mini-book – one might say a business biography – about you. Crafting it is more of an iterative process than a beginning-to-end marathon.

Every day, or several times a week, write a little more in "the book." This is another reason we recommend a word processor as an interim step to getting your profile actually posted up on LinkedIn.

Formatting Options are limited

LinkedIn profiles are rather bland when compared to their counterparts at Facebook, MySpace and the like. They are void of **bold**, <u>underline</u>, *italics*, font variations and even spelll checkkk.

This is why you will learn to really love your word processor. Use it to develop your text and then COPY and PASTE the text into your LinkedIn profile. LinkedIn is not without ANY formatting options, but it takes some knowhow to get the most out of it. We also have very clever tricks that we will share to show you how to use special graphics characters to dress up your profile text.

There are some formatting options you should be aware of as well. You can use ALL CAPS and any character available on your keyboard. For example! @ # $ % ^ & * ( ) - _ = + { } [ ] | \ " ' : ; ? / > . < , ~ `. You can still do a lot with upper case and lowercase letters, 10 digits, and these other standard keyboard characters. Here is a very clever idea from one of our readers:

```
....oooO...............
.....(....)...Oooo......
......)../.....(....)......
.....(_/.......)../.......
...............(_/.........
```

Tip! *LinkedIn allows a limited number of special characters to be inserted into LinkedIn profiles. Look at MY LinkedIn profile to see what I mean and how they might be used effectively in YOUR profile (www.linkedin.com/in/mikeoneil). In Microsoft Word, they can be found under "Symbols". Use the Word Help system to find out where they are in the menu structure. Here are some symbols that we recommend because they work well in LinkedIn:* | ▌ ◊ ► ◄↔ ♦ • ★ ☆

Breaking down your profile into components

Let's do a quick review of the areas of your LinkedIn profile and what information goes where. Here are the sections; you will find some great ideas on where to put specific profile information as we discuss each one.

- Name

- Headline

- Geographic Area (where you live)

- Industry (that you work in)

- Summary (text about you)

- Specialties (keywords about you)

- Experience (company, job title, period, description)

- Education (schooling)

- Additional Information (Websites, Twitter IDs, Interests, Groups and Associations, Personal Information)

- Contact Settings

We have included a nifty little tool we call the LinkedIn Profile Inventory in the back of this book. Use this Reference (Appendix A) to guide you through the steps to become familiar with what to expect. It guides you in building an inventory of keywords and phrases that actually help you brainstorm what information you need to build a Multi-Platinum profile.

Editing your Profile

LinkedIn makes it really easy to make edits to your Profile. You can do it from any page on LinkedIn. On the navigation bar, find the "Profile" text link. This will take you to a view of your Profile with edit text links sprinkled throughout that let you edit the individual sections.

When you hold (or hover) your mouse over the word "Profile," a drop-down menu appears offering you the option to jump right to "Edit Profile," "View Profile," or "Recommendations." When you view your own profile, you also have tabs above it to allow you to quickly jump between "Edit My Profile" and "View My Profile." I address recommendations in detail in Chapter 5 (Work Experience and Education) and Chapter 8 (The Dashboard.)

Your Name and Location – what do you call yourself?

While it seems simple, there are some rather significant strategies regarding your name. Are you Bob Plant or Robert Plant? Women have the biggest issues because of marriage. Carly Simon didn't become Carly Taylor and that was a good thing. That relationship didn't last long!

Lynyrd Skynyrd helps illustrate the point pretty well. I thought for awhile that it was spelled Leonard Skinnard. Did you?

When you created your LinkedIn profile, you were prompted to enter your name and location (your zip code). It might be time to review how your name is entered in the light of your "Profile Makeover." There are two ways to edit this information. From the Profile link, select "Edit Profile," then click the "edit" link beside your name. You can also access the "Name and Location" edit screen from the Account and Settings Screen (accessible from the "Settings" link at the top right side of any LinkedIn screen). Below "Personal Information" on the right column select "Name & Location."

Name

How simple is this? You can do FirstName LastName or FirstName LastInitial. We strongly suggest that you use FirstName LastName. See the screen shot below.

You will find people who complete the name field using different strategies to help them stand out or to be more easily found. Some put extra characters in

Basic Information

First Name:	Lori
Last Name:	Ruff
Former/Maiden Name:	Brunk 🔒
Display Name:	

    ⦿ Lori Ruff
    ○ Lori R.

Tip: For added Privacy, you can display only your first name and last initial. (Your connections will still see your first and last name.)

☑ Display LinkedIn account holder icon (in)

Professional "Headline": Speaker | Writer | National

Examples: Experienced Transportation Executive, Web Designer and Information Architect, Visionary Entrepreneur and Investor...See more

Country:	United States
Zip Code:	80202
Industry:	Professional Training & Coaching

Suggest a missing industry

Save Changes or Go back to Edit My Profile

Speak multiple languages?
You can create your profile in another language.
⊕ Create another profile

---

as part of their first name, last name, or both. They do this to gain attention, to encourage people to invite them and to appear at the top of search listings. These tricks are a little risky. They might affect your Google and LinkedIn since they are often looking for an exact match on the name.

Don't use special characters to begin your Last Name field, as this is how the LinkedIn address book sorts. Rather than putting you at the top of the list, this strategy will backfire and send you to the end of the contact list.

Marriages bring into question the need for Maiden and Former names. LinkedIn Profiles now accommodate a Maiden Name/Former Name field that appears as a Middle Name in Parenthesis. For example:

Lori (Brunk) Ruff

This option is only accessible from the Edit My Profile tab. When entering your maiden/former name, you will notice a tiny blue lock beside the text box. When you move your mouse over it, your pointer will change to a finger pointer. Click the lock and you will discover that LinkedIn gives you three options regarding whom you will allow to see your former/maiden name: Only Your Connections (Tier 1,) Your Network (1s, 2s, Groups, and 3s,) or Everyone. Lori recommends choosing everyone so that people who "knew you when" will be able to find you and know that they have the right person.

When crafting your name, headline and other fields, visit my LinkedIn profile; it is packed with tricks and with interesting applications and methodologies throughout. See it at www.linkedin.com/in/mikeoneil.

Even if you see other users who include special characters or their email address in their name field, like this:

Tom Smith tsmith@mycompany.com

or

! John Roberts LION TopLinked !

... don't do it! This extra information should go in the headline or contact information area. It is bad etiquette to use meaningless special characters, which serves little purpose and makes you less findable. Users may pass you by because of it. They want to clearly see who you are and know who they are know who they are potentially dealing with. If you try tricks that are deemed by most of the community as sneaky or underhanded, you will damage your credibility. Read on for more of our best practices!

Location

LinkedIn prompts you for a Zip Code so you can be assigned to a geographic area or region. Why is this important? In addition to letting people know where you are based (i.e., Abilene TX, Greater Denver Area or Netherlands), when you search on LinkedIn, your ZIP code determines the DEFAULT center or home base for the search. However you can always type over this default when doing searches that are geographic. The radius around the Zip Code defaults to 50 miles for all users and allows you to choose variations from ten to 100 miles.

Tip! *If you have a paid LinkedIn account (LinkedIn's pricing starts at $24.95 per month,) you can choose to display the Account Holder icon on your profile. Yes, you want to do this if you indeed have a paid account. It is part of what you are paying for and it adds credibility to you and your LinkedIn profile. You select this from the top of the Account and Settings area. There are more features being added to the LinkedIn Paid accounts annually as LinkedIn tries to coax more people into paying. Paid account features are covered later in the book.*

Your Industry –
What category are you in?

Remember this super popular band that came and went in the 80s? "Who can it be now?" I actually saw Men At Work in concert in Arizona during that little window of the band's popularity. Perhaps they brought together the concepts of work and Rock music for the first time?

Industry is a highly visible yet somewhat less important part of the LinkedIn Header area, even though it commands prime real estate on your LinkedIn profile. Many people feel that there is not a classification that fits them, even though there are well over 100 to choose from. You can suggest a new category to LinkedIn, but don't expect to see anything happen anytime soon. Check back every couple of months to see if they indeed added new industries, but be aware that this just is not a high priority for them.

Pick something from the list and get on with it. If you do SEO work (and they don't list SEO as an option), pick something related, like Internet. Just don't pick something that is inaccurate or misrepresents you. You must admit that you are certainly not a veterinarian if you are doing SEO work.

Here is a good idea - look at your top five or so competitors and see what they use. There is usually a consensus about which option to select. You can also look for companies in your industry that are not competitors, perhaps in other cities. Use the People Button and the LinkedIn search capabilities to find them. The Keyword search will be the main field you want to select to start the search.

In searches, one can elect to limit the search results to a specific industry or industries. Determining your industry is perhaps where this ability comes most into play, so it is somewhat important to spend a few minutes on it.

Your LinkedIn Headline – Your very best sound bite

"Shout it out loud"
- *KISS*

This where you want to focus your greatest attention, especially on a "per-character basis." You need to leap off the page with your "wordsmithing." If the song coming across your radio doesn't catch you in the first few chords, you might just go on to the next station. The same thing holds true for LinkedIn. The Headline is of particular importance, as it shows up in search results. A good one will attract people to look at your full profile.

The Headline is the first area encountered by a viewer, even before they see your Summary. It is brief (only 120 characters); an ever so important blurb that states what you do and what you are looking for. This is a VERY important area to nail down and take advantage of.

Why is the headline so important? Beyond your name, current company and current job title, it is the text that others see when you show up in search results. If your headline looks interesting, they may click through to your Profile to see more. If they do not find it appealing, it is off to the next person. Use as many of the 120 characters as possible.

 Tip! *If you type too many characters in any form field, LinkedIn will reject the change, indicate how many you are allowed, and tell you how many you have total. This is a nifty feature that keeps you from having to guess how much to trim.*

Here are some examples of "short" headlines:

- President, Strategic Systems LLC

- Business coach helping Entrepreneurs

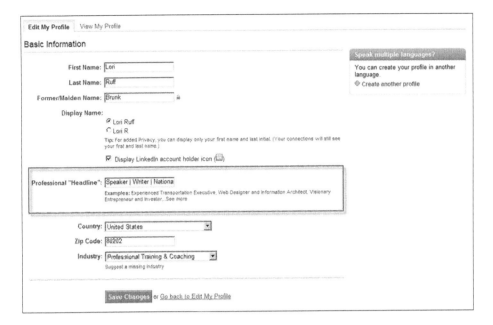

- Sr. Sales Manager, MCI

- Branch Manager, Phoenix, Cbeyond

- Executive Recruiter specializing in IT

Now, here are some more advanced headlines. Notice the difference:

- Public Speaker, Entrepreneur and Author of "The Total Idiot's Guide to Yahoo"

- CEO, CommonCraft Ventures LLC, investing in green energy concerns

- Sr. Development Manager, INFO for The Go, developers of mobile applications for the Oil and Gas Industry

- V.P. Sales, Sprint, covering West Coast Operations

- Chief Operating Officer (COO), Managed Hosting PLC, managed data center solutions for streaming media

Some might get even more advanced. Here are real headlines from real experts (found by searching on the LinkedIn keyword "expert"):

- Key Expert Work Injury and Rehabilitation at EU China Social Security Reform Co-operation Project

- EDI/B2B Process Expert, Business Development, Product Management and Wireless Mobile Computing Professional

- On-Air Talent, Lifestyle and Trend Expert, Author, Guest Speaker, Stylist

- SharePoint SME, Workflow Architect at John Wiley and Sons

And, of course, mine:

- The LinkedIn Rock Star, Social Media Authority, Speaker, Strategist, Author, Expert, #1 LinkedIn Trainer, 27,000+

Tip! *Look at other people's headlines to see what you like and what looks good for you. Look at people in similar occupations to see what they are doing. You AT LEAST want to be as good as these people, and hopefully much better. Check around with friends (those on LinkedIn) who know you professionally and ask what they think.*

Using your word processor, create several different headlines and see how they look. After spell checking, pick the best one and cut and paste it into the data entry field for Headlines. You might want to rotate the Headline periodically to test various versions. You will find yourself eventually choosing a favorite.

If you would like to continue on, you might put in something that "fits" for now and come back later to modify it. A job title, the company name, and a few things about your role will do for now.

Your Photo –
The Hood Ornament

"Kodachrome"
Paul Simon

"Photograph"
Def Leppard

Remember buying an album from an unknown band without hearing any of the music on it? (The keyword here is "unknown," of course.) I do. If I could hear the music, perhaps at a listening station or on the radio, it was another story. Now you are talking! Fast forward to the digital music world of today and you get the idea of how much more we demand now.

Because they are already well-known or among my favorite bands, I don't have to listen to know that I want the next Pink Floyd or Luce album (www.luceband.com). They have a brand and their visual image is a part of their brand. It was bands like Def Leppard and music videos that really brought the visual element through the new medium of MTV. Remember?

When someone does a search and your profile shows up in the results, your picture is part of what is shown: or not. Your picture can influence a click-through to your profile as much as anything except perhaps your headline.

Let's use a simple metaphor. Have you ever been on a blind date? How much difference does a picture make in a no/no-go decision? Business isn't much different, especially not in the modern world of social media, where we expect to be able be able to learn more online.

How inclined are you to create a business relationship with someone you can't see? Ever wonder if Pat (of SNL fame) were a man or a woman? Not having a picture makes it look like 1) you forgot, 2) you couldn't figure out how to do it, or 3) you didn't think it was important. All of those are reasons for someone to pass you by in favor of a more complete profile. After all, there are often many from which to choose.

Do you have a professional or good quality JPG, GIF or PNG photo of yourself? A headshot or ¾ pose? If not, please arrange to have one made as people want to do business with people they know and trust. A photo goes a long way to enabling people to feel comfortable connecting with you!

While it is always best to have a professional headshot, the size of this photo is small (80X80 pixels) so it is not as important here as elsewhere. We recommend a white background and a clear photo of your smile. A good cell phone camera shot can suffice until you have something else better.

What you are trying to convey with your photo is that you are credible, approachable and helpful. It should reflect your status or profession. For example, a friend who is a photographer has a headshot of himself holding his camera. You can still see his eyes but it is clear from his photo that he is serious about his profession. "That is the person I want taking my picture!"

When you upload your photo, crop it as close into your face as you can. It needs to show a real person who is approachable and willing to help.

Here are some examples:

These users can be found on LinkedIn at http://www.LinkedIn.com/in/ USERNAME (below):

/Fuelvm   */ShawnWalker*

/BobTodd   */NancyLaine*   */NeilMcKenziePhoto*

To upload your photo:

1. Click on "Edit Your Photo" in the header area to the right of your name field.

2. Select "Choose File," browse to the photo you want to import. It needs to be less than 4 MB. The end result will only be 80x80 pixels.

3. Click "Upload Photo" and then use the cropping tool to zoom in or move the visible region of the photo.

4. Choose who you want to see your photo ... My Connections; My Network; or Everyone. We recommend selecting "Everyone."

5. Click "Save Settings."

And of course the authors' LinkedIn photos (courtesy of **www.NeilMckenziePhotography.com**):

/LoriRuff

/MikeOneil

Your Status – "What are you working on now?"

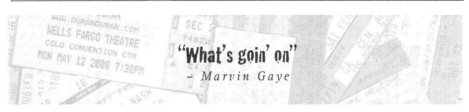

"What's goin' on"
– Marvin Gaye

LinkedIn's status field has counterparts in Twitter, Facebook and other platforms. It is NOT the same thing, however. It's about "what's goin' on" this week or this month, not this very minute. For example – "the band is in the studio working on (cutting) their next album," not "laying down that hot new track."

This interesting update feature actually comes from another program called Twitter. You can tell people what you are currently up to and it is part of the upper header area as shown in Item 2. Here Lori Ruff says: *Rock the World with Your Online Presences Book now available. IT ROCKS!*

Change it weekly so it is fresh and others will pay more attention to it. You can copy/paste with the SAME EXACT TEXT if you like. It will still look "fresh." If you have elected to share your status updates, others will get a notification when it is changed – a good way to keep yourself top of mind.

Whatever you write, keep it businesslike and of interest to others. After all, LinkedIn asks you "What are you *working on* now?" and not "What are you *doing* now?"

There are several places to actually see and update your status:

1. The LinkedIn Home Page. Your status is displayed right in the middle, where it is easy to see and change.

2. The LinkedIn Profile. In Profile Edit Mode, you can see your current status and make changes. In Profile View Mode, you can only see it.

3. You are now able to connect your LinkedIn Status to one or more Twitter accounts. When updating your Network Status from your LinkedIn home page, simply check the box below the Status

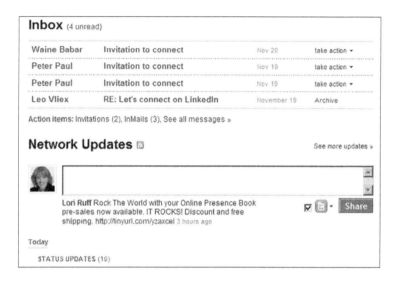

entry field (to the left of the Twitter icon.) If you have connected multiple Twitter accounts to your LinkedIn profile, simply click the drop-down arrow on the right of the Twitter icon and select which Twitter account you wish to update. Then click the Share button.

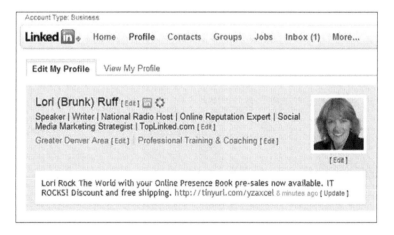

You can access your Twitter Settings from the drop-down arrow on the right of the Twitter icon or from the Settings link at the top of your screen. From Settings, look under Profile Settings and select the last option titled "Twitter Settings." In addition to adding and removing your Twitter accounts, you may select which account you want to provide access to update your LinkedIn network status. LinkedIn provides two options – 1) share all tweets (I do not recommend this) or share only tweets that contain #in (read as "hashtag in").

The importance of this communication integration cannot be overstated. The brilliance of this feature is your ability to selectively and strategically coordinate status communications between your LinkedIn and Twitter "networks" in either one or both directions (from LinkedIn to Twitter and/or Twitter to LinkedIn.)

Tip! *Use your LinkedIn Network Status to let others know of the PROJECTS you are working on. The shelf life might be a week to a month. On the other hand, use Twitter to let others know "what you are doing now" that might be of interest to them. Twitter is about finding relationships through conversation; LinkedIn is for creating and maintaining business relationships through networking and interaction.*

For more details about the Twitter application, see Chapter 8 (Account and Settings) and Chapter 9 (LinkedIn Applications).

Your Public Profile - what should others get to see

"See Me, Feel me"
- *The Who*

"Invisible Touch"
- *Genesis*

When bands go to a studio to cut a record, they use lots of mixing equipment to get it just right. Everything is cut in raw form, then refined, then mixed and then released. See (just the right amount of) me, Feel (just the right amount of) me. With all the music recorded, they decide what makes it into the final cut for the outside world. You see, LinkedIn profiles are fully indexed by search engines and can show up in searches from the likes of Google, Yahoo, Bing, or MSN.

If you prefer an "Invisible Touch", you can turn off some or all of your profile from the world. It would only be searchable and findable from within the LinkedIn community. In either case, the LinkedIn search system still sees all the text you put in your profile. The power is there, you may want to just "turn it all on baby."

LinkedIn lets you determine exactly what is visible (or invisible) when others look at your LinkedIn profile from outside of LinkedIn (for example, if your profile comes up in an Internet search from Google or Yahoo). You can choose to be totally invisible, to show others selected sections of your information, or to choose every area of your LinkedIn profile that can be viewed by others. In general, you want people to see you. That is why you are here in the first place, isn't it? Remember that they cannot see your contact settings or personal information until they log into the system and, in the case of personal information, actually connect with you.

Here are the options:

None

This will hide your profile from the view of everyone doing a web search. It is as if you are not even there as far as others finding you and seeing your profile. However, when people log into LinkedIn, they can find your profile.

If you have your name set to first name, last initial, and your Public Profile set to "None," people within LinkedIn but outside of your network will see "PRIVATE" in place of your name.

Basic Profile

The Basic Profile shows only your Name, Industry, Location and the Number of Recommendations you have.

Full Profile Options

The Full Profile lets you choose which areas you wish to have on display. All the items in the Basic Profile (Name, Industry, Location and the Number of Recommendations) are automatically included, as well as your choice of any or all of the following:

- Headline
- Summary
- Specialties
- Current Positions – with or without details
- Past Positions - with or without details
- Educations - with or without details
- Websites
- Interests
- Groups
- Honors and Awards
- Interested in... (why people should contact you).

The illustration shows you what the Public Profile screen looks like and how the check boxes work.

I highly suggest that you include all of the items listed in the Full Profile, unless there is a good reason not to. The question you should ask is "Why Not?" vs. "Why?"

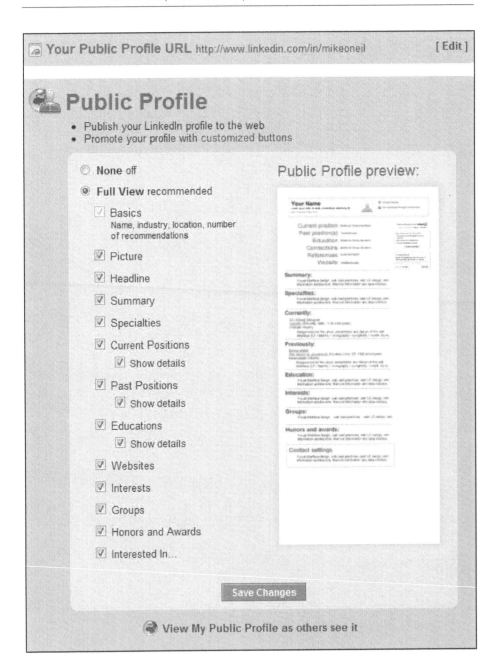

Your Profile Summary –
showing others how well you
can you write

"Don't stop thinking about tomorrow"
- *Fleetwood Mac*

"Livin' in the past"
- *Jethro Tull*

"What you need"
- *INXS*

The Summary Section is about the future, about "tomorrow." It isn't about "Livin' in the past." It should highlight, in concise terminology, what you can do for others going forward. It is, in an 80/20 sense, 80 percent what you can do and 20 percent "what you need" (what others can do to help you).

Think of it as a remake of a classic song (or two) such as Kid Rock reworking Lynyrd Skynyrd and Warren Zevon music into a new song "All Summer Long" (2009).

After the Headline, the Summary is the single most important part of your profile. This is where you should spend most of the time and attention. DO NOT simply paste in your resume. A resume typically looks 90 percent backward and ten percent forward. Your LinkedIn profile is much the opposite. It is almost all forward-looking, even the history! If your headline is the attention grabber that draws people to your profile, your Summary gives you a great chance of establishing credibility with them once they arrive and start to read. This is your opportunity to "control your professional identity." [3]

You have about 2/3 of a printed page to develop the Summary Section (2,000 characters) and you should eventually use most of it when you are done with your profile. LinkedIn will tell you how many characters you have entered and how many you have left when you cut and paste text here. That's a really nifty feature.

Within the Summary section itself, the first few paragraphs are the most important just like a newspaper article and many other types of published text. There are a lot of ways to start out a profile. Some are basic and simple. Let's start out there - nice and simple.

The first 1/4 or 1/3 of your summary is for people visiting your profile to BECOME INTERESTED IN YOU if they fit the audience you are looking for. That is who you are writing this for—not the general public—so be specific to attract your target audience. Write a short paragraph about who you are and what you have to offer; what value do you bring the reader? It is okay if what you write turns some people away. They are self-opting out and will do so without interrupting your day with questions that will result in "no sale" anyway!

The next 1/3 of your summary should be about your company:

Work for a mid-to-large company? Try some information on your company first perhaps.

- What they do

- Where they do it

- Who their customers are

- What makes them special

Work for a small company (not self employed)? Make it a little less about the organization.

- What they do

- Who their customers are

[3] http://www.LinkedIn.com

- What makes them special

Self employed or work for yourself? It becomes more about you.

- Your role as the "chief" and what makes you special?

- What does your product or service do?

- How did you get to this point? What is it about your past that lends credibility to what you do now?

Next, give people a wrap-up of your background as it pertains to today and to the future. What have you done that matters NOW? Use short sentences with two to three sentences per paragraph. Each paragraph should be no more than five or six lines so that you employ white space and keep it readable.

If you have done things that are relevant going forward – experiences, projects, contacts, etc. – this is good to include next (the last third or so of the Summary.) The key here is what you are doing NOW and that it is relevant. You might then wrap up with what inspires you, what you like to do when you are not in the center of your business universe it is nice to finish with something personal. Keep it simple and concise.

This is important because it begins to build the relationship you are looking for. Even before people talk to you personally they can read your Profile and gain a sense of knowing who you are and how you can help them. If it is appropriate, they will want to contact you to continue the relationship. Perhaps resulting in business.

 Tip! *Use action words and not typical descriptive text. Remember, there are tens of millions of people on LinkedIn and you want to look special in this important crowd.*

I suggest you consider buying the book **Words that Sell** *by Richard Bayan. It makes use of the colorful part of the English language.*

For example - are you "experienced" or are you a "seasoned veteran" or an "industry expert?" You get the idea. This book is a super thesaurus for just this purpose. There are other variants of this book, and they are very good as well.

Another good source for ideas on words is **www.Thesaurus.com**. *I use it all the time. BOTH were used in the writing and titling of this book!*

Let me use an analogy to illustrate why words can be so important.

- When you were in high school, maybe you were near the top of your class. Then you went to college and were maybe average. The same analogy works for sports, from high school or college to the pros. The reason is that the field is larger and the competition is greater.

- So now you are on LinkedIn and that definitely sets you apart. You have an edge over all those people that are NOT on LinkedIn. On the flip side, you are now part of millions and millions of LinkedIn users. The analogy above has some meaning here as well.

Why do I bring this up? Well, this is a pep talk aimed at inspiring you to make your LinkedIn profile special – or even better, perhaps a bit "sexy." There is still competition out there on LinkedIn. Some people stand out and some do not. It is easy to get lost in the shuffle. Our most powerful tool on LinkedIn is words, so how do we "stand out" using only words?

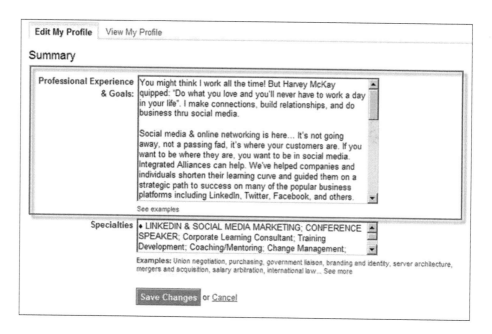

Your Specialties – a place to list your keywords

"We've only just begun"
– The Carpenters

You are not done with the Summary section. It actually has a commonly overlooked cousin called Specialties. While the Summary section is among the most important places for the human eye, the Specialties section is among the most important for the computer's "eye." This section is designed to be read by the search engine within LinkedIn. As such, it isn't about flowing sentences and colorful adjectives. Don't worry, the computers won't be offended.

Below the LinkedIn Summary is Specialties. You probably have a lot of things in your background that are best shown in a bulleted or comma-separated listing. Use the Specialties section for this. It is best for words and not sentences. You can use commas, bullets, semi-colons – it is pretty open to variability. You have a couple of paragraphs of space to work with (500 characters.)

Do NOT repeat the information from the Summary in Specialties. It is often used for listings of areas of expertise, particular products you have worked with, additional certifications, etc., and it usually appears as a listing with words separated by commas.

For example, you might list:

speak, speaker, speaking, train, trainer, training, author, writer...

Get the idea? You need keywords and variations of those keywords. If you only list "speaker" and a search is done looking for someone who does "speaking," the computer will not find you!

There are a couple of strategies here that may work for you. If you are doing new things now, but your past is still relevant, consider heading two paragraphs: "current" and "past." For example, I have a strong background as a sales engineer in the technology and telecom fields. I am now one of the leading authorities on LinkedIn and social media. My past does affect my ability to deliver effective training and social media strategic consulting to the industries in which I spent so many years.

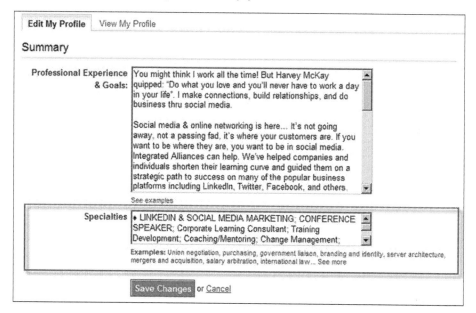

On the other hand, if you have spent your career mostly in the same field or industry, you might use one large paragraph of keywords and variations of those keywords, so the list is more for findability during searches than for anything else. Keep in mind, though, that this is still an area that is likely to be read more than anything below this point, so make it readable.

Keyword Inventory

In its most fundamental element, there are two basic reasons people use LinkedIn – to find and to be found. In the Profile section, we went over being found. Focus on the fact that you are creating an attraction strategy from your headline to your summary to all the keywords. Your goal is to enable people to locate your profile so they can determine if they want to do business with you.

When people are looking for someone like you, they typically use the LinkedIn Search screen. In most cases, they search on one of more of the following criteria, listed in decreasing order of importance:

- Keywords

- Name

- Job titles

- Companies

Knowing this, you might think that a little extra attention to keywords is probably a good thing, and you would be right. Let's go over some strategies.

Take a look at things from the perspective of the user who might be trying to find you. What words would they use to find you from among the millions of LinkedIn users? Think in terms of their finding you for the purpose that you wish to be found.

Step one is to strategize and write down all the words and phrases you wish to be found under. Does this sound like Search Engine Optimization (SEO) for a Website? You bet! Some good ways to find new words are to ask your newest customers how they found you. What were they thinking of when they went looking for someone like you? You want to ask your new customers, because they haven't learned your language yet.

Also, if you have a Google AdWords account, what are the words that you use in it? Make sure those are in your profile. What about your competitors? How are they found? What words or phrases are in their profile that fit you well? If they show up in search results, wouldn't you want to show up too? At least with them, if not ahead of them!

 Tip! *Put these words in Microsoft Word or Excel one per line. Then use the thesaurus function to see what other words might fit. Add them to the list. These are the words that you want to weave throughout your Profile. Once you have your list, show it to others who know you and whom you trust. Ask them what you missed.*

Assembling your story

Now you are ready to write a short paragraph about who you are and what you have to offer. What value do you bring the reader?

Remember that the next 1/3 of your summary should be about your company and your role there, including perhaps what the company culture is like.

Next, give people an overview of your background as it pertains to today and to the future. What have you done that matters NOW? Use short sentences with two to three sentences per paragraph. Each paragraph should be no more than five to six lines so that you employ white space and keep it readable.

Again, remember that if there are things you have done that are relevant going forward – experiences, projects, contacts, etc. – this is a good place to include them (the last third or so of the Summary.) The key here is to focus on what you are doing NOW and keep it relevant.

You might then wrap up with what inspires you, what you like to do when you are not in the center of your business universe, something personal. Again, keep it simple and concise.

Your Work Experience – What jobs have you held?

"Old Days"
– *Chicago*

"Are you Experienced?"
– *Jimi Hendrix*

New business relationships are often formed based on your past work history. The further you go back and input your past employment, the better your chances of making more relationships and the BETTER those relationships might become. Isn't it a bonding experience talking about the good old days? "Old Days, good times I remember." "Are you experienced" in some ways other than college? These experiences count too. Put them in! Include volunteer and paid positions to gain the most benefit.

The Experience Section of the LinkedIn Profile is where there are some parallels to a traditional resume. It is tempting to paste in what you have on your resume. It really depends on what that looks like as to whether or not it should change much. In most cases, it needs major surgery versus a cut-and-paste.

 Tip! *Keep in mind, that no matter how you adapt it – the information MUST agree with your resume.*

If you want to fast-start, use the resume text for now. You want to get basic information in here and then go back and refine it. Unless you also use the included LinkedIn Profile Inventory (Appendix A) or the worksheet available at **www.RockTheWorldBook.com/Extras,** do not forget to go back and update your profile to make it forward-looking. Remember that your past should strengthen your claim of experience today.

Be careful when adding a new "Current" position, because there is a checkbox that allows LinkedIn to update your Headline with the title and company name. UNCHECK THIS BOX! You don't want to customize your headline just to have LinkedIn default back to the standard boilerplate stuff everyone else is using.

Below is the screen for adding a position. When you type in the name of the company, it will try and match it up with a company already in the sys-

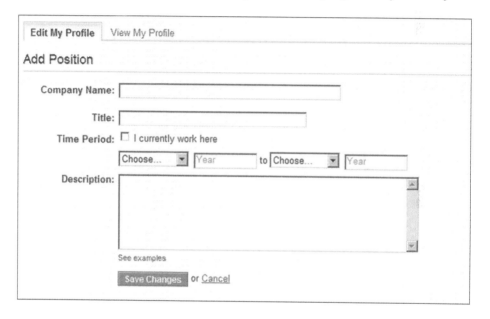

tem. If you can highlight a company and press enter, it will fill in a number of fields for you – Website, Industry, Size (# of employees.)

If the company name is not in the list, you can add it. Here is the information that LinkedIn will ask you for:

1. Job Title

2. Company/Organization Name

3. Start and End Dates
    (month and year)

4. Description of the Position

Drilling down a bit deeper, we have some strategies, advice and best practices for you.

Include all of your employers/jobs/significant volunteer positions. If you had multiple titles at the same company and they were in different areas, put the job in twice (yes, two jobs at the same company, but in a series.) Only list the highest position you held in a particular area (i.e., Sales Manager versus Sales Rep. and THEN Sales Manager.)

Feel free to put yourself in the best possible light – Sr. Account Executive sounds a lot better than Sales Rep. However, make sure that the words you chose accurately represent your title and your role at the company. Again, your Profile, which is peer-reviewed, should agree with your resume.

 You have 100 characters for the Title field; include acronyms and variations of your title to make it easier for people to find you. For example, you might include "VP | Vice President", or "Sales Representative; Account Manager; Business Relationship Manager." You can and should include your formal as well as popular descriptive titles to ensure that you show up more often in search results. After all, the Title field is one with high SEO value!

The more recent positions should have most of the following information included with jobs further in your past having just some of this information as it applies to the work that you do today. Each position allows you 2,000 characters ... use them and make them rich with keywords that will enable people to find you.

For each job, add the following information in the "Description of Position" section:

*   What the company did (what they made, sold, etc.)

*   Who they did it for if it isn't obvious (industry, type of account, level at a company)

*   Where THEY or YOU "did it" if it isn't obvious (region)

*   What your role there was

- Anything important relating to what you do today

- Anything amazing that you did or that happened when you were there

Make it exciting and important, but do NOT use statistics like you might on a resume. Few people care if you made 221 percent of quota in 1998. They do want to know if you did international work or led a division or region or if you had a staff of X number of people reporting to you. If you have or had a side business, put it in as a job, perhaps a "concurrent job." As you insert the dates, LinkedIn will order the positions according to start date.

Your company name seems simple, and for most people it is. In business today it is commonplace to use abbreviations, variations and shortenings of the company name. Consider all of the options and do some searching on your own to see how others from the same company spell it. Use the most popular standard that you find to be sure you are properly affiliated.

The Work Period is just as it sounds and it is important for two particular reasons – the LinkedIn Colleagues feature and reference searches, both of which you will learn about later. Just include the years employed when LinkedIn asks you for the start and end dates.

It is not necessary to include months unless you want to ensure certain positions appear in a certain order. LinkedIn shows jobs, whether past or current, ordered by start date. If you have concurrent positions with the same start date, then you need to enter the data for the one you want to appear first last!

Take care that your work period dates agree with the dates on your resume(s). It is typically acceptable to fudge dates of less important experiences in order to be sure the more important position is listed first; but use care or be prepared to disclose why you changed the date.

Your Education – where and what you have learned

"School's out"
– *Alice Cooper*

"My Old School"
– *Steely Dan*

Even if you didn't finish some schooling or just took a few classes, it belongs in your LinkedIn profile. "I know a little" adds up in the minds of others. Go all the way back to high school – to "My Old School." It gives you another place to create bonds with others.

The Education section is another area where the profile looks a bit like a resume. We suggest that you list all of your schools, including high school. If you went for two semesters or more, list it. If you took classes that are relevant to what you do today, list them too. Dale Carnegie – sure, include it. What else is there?

If you did anything special at these institutions, list it. If you were in a fraternity, sorority, sport, interest group, etc., put it in. You have 500 characters in Activities and Societies and 1,000 for Additional Notes! Talk about why your education then is relevant to your expertise now. Pack it with keywords you want to be found on.

Tip! *We highly suggest that you do this for every educational experience. Even if you took one class or seminar at a college; adding it will allow you to join LinkedIn Alumni Groups.*

There are a few strategies that you can use to get the most out of education.

Degree – While you can only see 20 characters at a time, you actually have 100 characters to work with. That is enough to put in a full degree name like "BS Industrial Engineering and Management Systems" or even something much larger. Just don't use any more characters than you need or it can be difficult for viewers to read.

Field(s) of Study – If you had other significant areas that you studied, put them in here. Some examples might be "International Trade" or "Discreet Electronics."

Dates Attended – Like the job dates, this is relatively significant. LinkedIn has a feature called Classmates that matches you up with other people you went to school with. Some people have put in their educational experience and left off the dates so they could search for other alumni without being restricted by the years of their own attendance.

If you are worried that the dates you were in school might age you, don't be. Remember the LinkedIn demographic? The average-aged user of 41+ appreciates grey hair a bit (or a lot.)

Activities and Societies Subsection – If you were part of any group (fraternity, sorority, clubs, sports, etc.) put this information here separated by commas. The commas indicate the start and stop of a clickable keyword. Each word or phrase you enter here becomes a hotlink to an instant search within LinkedIn IF THE COMMAS ARE PUT IN PROPERLY. Simply enter the words and phrases separated by commas like this:

Phi Theta Kappa, Honor Society, graduated Cum Laude, Chess Club, Students Against Drunk Driving, GPA 3.96

To understand how this works, enter the information. Then go to "View Your Profile." You will see that all of these words and phrases are hotlinks so that, when you click them, LinkedIn performs a search of that keyword or phrase and allows you to find other people with the same word or phrase in their profile. If no one else comes up in the search, try modifying the information until you find other people. This is a great way to search for other users with whom you already have something in common (connect with them!), as well as to be more findable when others perform those searches.

Additional Notes – Was there anything especially noteworthy about your experience? Put it here. This is a good place to tell a story about why you picked the major or industry that you did. Also, why your education proved to be relevant to the work you do now. If your education was a while ago, start with something like: "I didn't realize it at the time, but..." The point is you have 1,000 characters to work with here, so pack the space with more keywords that will allow people to find you through your profile by searching LinkedIn.

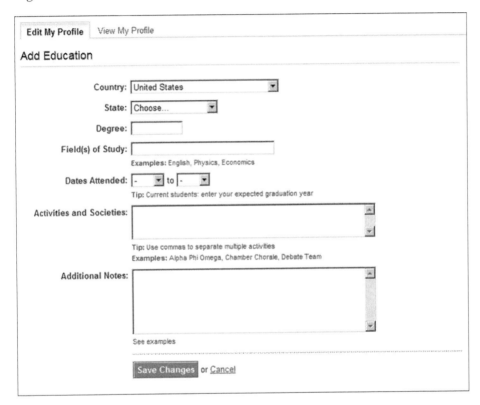

LinkedIn Recommendations – people endorse you and your work

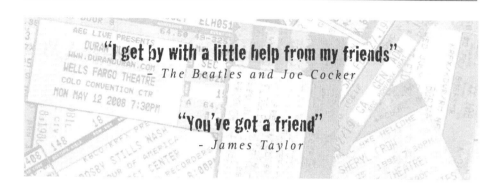

"I get by with a little help from my friends"
— *The Beatles and Joe Cocker*

"You've got a friend"
- *James Taylor*

Recommendations say that you are worthy. While it is not simply a "friends" thing, your friends who have come from business relationships are among the best places to start. As I look around, at least three out of four of my friends come from business or some extension of my business life. How about you? Can you say "You've got a friend?"

LinkedIn lets you get recommendations (endorsements or testimonials) from others, and they can receive recommendations from you. A recommendation is a vote of confidence in you, so strive to get a minimum of five to 15 recommendations. In fact, your profile is not considered 100 percent complete by LinkedIn until you have at least three recommendations. As you enter your experience and education, consider who might write a good recommendation for you for each of those positions.

Your recommendations should not be focused on you as a "person" so much as on your performance at a specific employer or educational institution. In fact, the recommendations are associated with specific positions. Ask people from whom you are seeking recommendations to tell a story about a project that you worked on together and your significance to the success of that project. If they can inject some numbers into the story it is even better. Here is an example:

"Mike led a project where we brought up telecom services for eight offices over a long weekend. Mike's hard work and expert planning let the project go off without a hitch. We simply couldn't have done it without him. I highly recommend Mike if you want things done right!"

Try to get recommendations from a variety of people, and keep them to three to five sentences in length. Those with higher-level job titles (President, VP, etc.), even at small companies, are the best sources of recommendations. Next best are those individuals who worked for well-known companies (household names) but at lower-level positions.

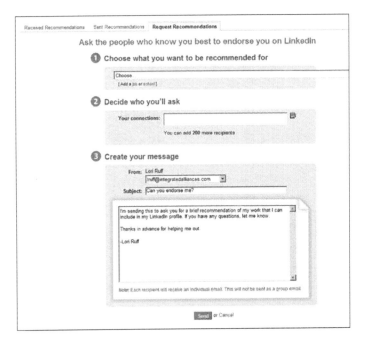

Recommend others. They will automatically be prompted to return the favor for you once they accept. This also puts your writing sample on THEIR profile with a link back to your profile. You can recommend someone by going to their profile and clicking on the text link "Recommend this person" to the right of their picture and/or their name, near the top of the screen.

 You do not have to be connected with someone to recommend them; however, you do in order to ask them for a recommendation through LinkedIn. If you are not connected, you could email them with a link to your profile and instructions to click the "recommend this person" beside your picture.

Manage Recommendations

Here you will see each of your positions and educational experiences with links to help you manage your recommendations.

If you have Received Recommendations for a position, you will see the total number of recommendations for that position, how many you have made visible, how many are hidden, and how many pending requests you have. You will also see this link:

[Manage | Ask to be endorsed]

If you have no recommendations, it will say so and you will see this link:

[Ask to be endorsed]

Below the list of positions and education, you will see a link to Add a job | Add a school. This takes you to the same place as when you select these links from the Edit My Profile screen.

Make a recommendation

At the bottom, you have a form available to "Make a recommendation."

You simply put in the first and last name, the email, and then indicate whether you are recommending the person as a Colleague, Service Provider, Business Partner or Student. Click "Continue."

If the recommendation is for a Service Provider, complete a form to indicate the position you're recommending the person for, the service category, the year first hired. A checkbox indicates if you've hired this person more than once. Also choose three attributes from a list to describe the person you are recommending.

If it is for a colleague, business partner, or student, you have different options. For a colleague or student, you will select the basis for the recommendation. That is, what was your relationship to this person? For a colleague, was this a direct reporting relationship, or did you work with them in the same or a different group? For students, were you their teacher, or advisor, or did you study with them? Next you will select your title and the other person's title (select each of these options from drop-down menus) "at the time" you knew them, which will be the period covered by your recommendation.

Now, you have to actually write a concise yet descriptive recommendation. Finally, you will see a link at the bottom to [view/edit] a message to be sent with your recommendation. "I've written this recommendation of your work to share with other LinkedIn users." This is OK to leave, but you may want to personalize the message and then click "send." You will see a message: "Your (type) recommendation has been created" at the top of your screen.

 Tip! *Recommendations you make or receive shown on your member feed and on the network update of your connections.*

At the top of this list, in the bar entitled "Recommendations," you will notice that there are three tabs: Received Recommendations, Sent Recommendations, and Request Recommendations. The "Received Recommendations" tab is highlighted. Click on "Sent Recommendations" to see the listing of recommendations you have sent. You can filter the list by type; you can edit each, and you can indicate to whom you want each displayed. Also, the date on which you made the recommendation is displayed.

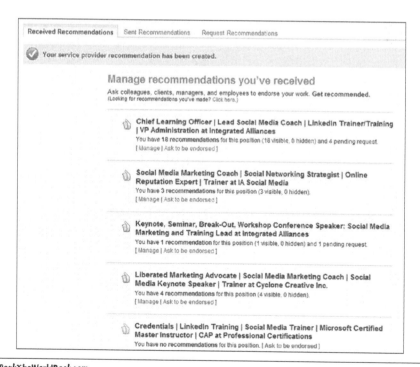

Request a recommendation

Whether you click the link to "Ask to be endorsed," or the tab "Request Recommendations," you are brought to the same screen. Complete a simple form to start the process. First, select the position or school experience for which you want to be recommended. Next, choose which LinkedIn connections you want to receive the request. You can either start typing each name, selecting the appropriate connection from the list that appears, or click the LinkedIn Address Book icon to the right of the dialog box and choose connections in the Choose Connections dialog box. Click the Finish button when you are done. You can send this request to up to 200 connections at one time.

Select which email you want the recommendation to come from. This is important when you have multiple email addresses associated with your LinkedIn account, because it helps people recognize who the request is coming from. You may want this to come from a personal or professional email account. If you use a separate email for your LinkedIn communications, this gives you the option for people to respond to an alternate address.

Next, you have the option to customize the subject line and message text. I recommend that you keep the default subject text so that people recognize it easily. However, I do recommend that you customize the message text to assist your connections with the recommendation. Remember that a specific recommendation is preferable rather than just getting a general "pat on the back" recommendation. Make it easy for people to recommend you by letting them know what you want to be recommended for. I have even seen people write a draft for the connections to start with. If you make it easy for people, they are more likely to respond in a positive way.

It is important to note that you can only request recommendations from current 1st tier connections. If you want to receive recommendations from others, it is better to send them a request via email with a link to your profile and instructions on how to submit a recommendation. Tell them to start by clicking the link beside your picture!

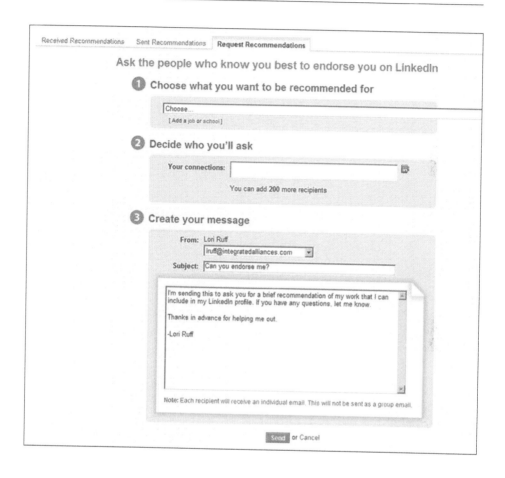

In Review

Remember that your LinkedIn profile is NOT a resume. However, your resume is not a bad place to start. Don't worry, if you have not written a resume in years; you're not that far behind.

Tip! *We recommend listing all of your current occupations and significant volunteer activities as long as they support your message. If you are a CPA who also sells life insurance, that's OK. If you are a lawyer who also sells Mary Kay, leave out the less-lucrative career.*

Tip! *Although you may copy and paste or upload your resume to help answer these questions, keep in mind that your LinkedIn profile is more than a resume. It should be forward-thinking, more like a brochure or extensive marketing piece.*

Tip! *Breaking down the components you will need for each experience, answer the questions found on the worksheet available at* **www.RockTheWorldBook.com/Extras.** *Make multiple copies of this so you have one for each current position, each previous position, and each significant educational experience.*

Tip! *If former companies no longer exist, or if they have merged with or been acquired by other companies, put the names of the companies when you worked there and also note the current names. Search LinkedIn for both, and see where you will gain the most exposure. If you use the current company name, in the description you can indicate "formerly..."*

Additional Information – the rest of the story

"Like to get to know you well"
– *Howard Jones*

Your personal side tells people a lot about you as an individual. Remember, this is a business site so you need to keep it within some limits. What is there about you that you wish to share that others will look favorably upon? ...Movies, music, hobbies, travels – yes. Dislikes, turnoffs, your wild side – no.

This is a sort of catch-all section for things that are not specific to other areas. Other than the Websites, all of this information ONLY appears near the bottom of your profile when others view it.

- Websites

- Interests

- Groups & Associations

- Honors & Awards

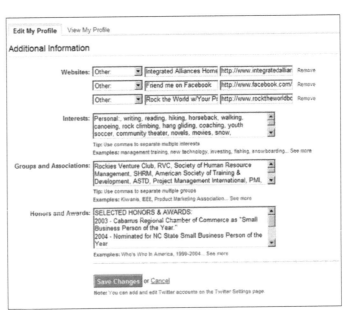

Your Websites – click here to find out more

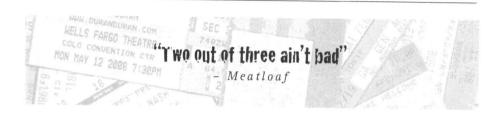

"Two out of three ain't bad"
– *Meatloaf*

Don't stop with one website. Get two or three in there even if they just point to subpages on the same website. Got a blog site or a Facebook page? If so, that adds up to three pretty quickly doesn't it? Remember to change the label (explained below.) "My website" doesn't inspire most people to click.

If you work for a company that has a website, by all means use it. If you have your own website, use it. Some people will put in a personal Website. Consider this only if it is relevant to your purpose for being on LinkedIn. If there are sub-pages on a website you want to direct people to (a jobs board, a sign-up page, etc.), this is a good place to use it.

LinkedIn gives you room to put in up to three Website addresses. Go ahead and use all three. LinkedIn offers the following titles for your Website addresses.

- My website

- My Company

- My Blog

- My RSS Feed

- My Portfolio

- Other:

When entering website information, always select "Other" and include your own label. Suggestions would be "Company Name" or "Learn more about me" or "See examples of my Work" or even "Search our Jobs."

If you are a member of an affiliate program, you can list it here. For example, if you were an affiliate for Integrated Alliances, you could insert a text label like, "Find LinkedIn Training Here" and then the website URL would take people to the training sub-page at our website For example, www.integratedalliances.com/training.

Some of our experts at Integrated Alliances work to turn the connections they make on LinkedIn into relationships. They do this by entering: "Friend Me On Facebook" in their website listings. They point these to their profiles on other social networking platforms so that people can connect with them in multiple locations, understanding that each has a different purpose.

Interests –
what strikes your fancy

"The real me"
– The Who

"True Colors"
– Cyndi Lauper

This is where you get to be yourself, to show the "Real" you, to show your "True Colors." Let other people see the things that you like to do; let them see what type of a person you really are. It helps create relationships with others in a whole new area. Mention muscle cars or Classic Rock and you got my attention. What gets you excited?

These are personal interests for the most part (golf, skiing, classic cars, traveling, etc.) List them in the order of what is most important to you. Be sure to list the words or phrases separated by commas. Each word or phrase you enter here becomes a hotlink to an instant search within LinkedIn IF THE COMMAS ARE PUT IN PROPERLY. It is much like the Activities and Societies section of your Education, these are working hot links. Remember that you only see the links when you "View My Profile," not in Edit mode.

Why care about interests? This is a business tool, right? Look at it this way – when you share an interest with someone else, it can be a very good thing. People are obviously interested in that thing and so are you (or it would not be listed).

Don't be afraid to put in your favorite artist or your favorite car. People you might do business with are more likely to connect with you if you have a common interest. When you start with a common bond, it changes the conversation. Instead of trying to figure out how to work together, you have something interesting to talk about, which will lead to an emotional attachment that will encourage people to want to do business with you instead of your competitor.

Groups and Associations – professional affiliations

"A matter of trust"
– Billy Joel

Carefully selecting the right Groups and Associations here (and in the LinkedIn Groups Section) will add to your credibility. It lets their good brand rub off a little bit on you. Doesn't the opening band get a form of this credibility by association with the band they are opening for?

This is another Hot Link Searchable section. If you are a member of any professional associations or groups, this is where to put that information. Put the name in, separated by commas, followed by any acronyms or abbreviations that the organizations use. As elsewhere, each word or phrase you enter here becomes a hotlink to an instant search within LinkedIn IF THE COMMAS ARE PUT IN PROPERLY.

For example: American Society for Training & Development, ASTD. Both American Society for Training & Development, and ASTD are clickable ho links. Also notice that we chose the ampersand "&" rather than spelling out the word "and." To the LinkedIn search engine, "and" and the ampersand are now interchangeable.

As you complete each section of your profile, look at "View My Profile" to see how other LinkedIn users will see it. Also do searches on the hot linked words and phrases to see what comes up. If no one else or very few people are using that key word or phrase, it might be a waste of space in a hot-linked area of your profile. Put it somewhere else and save the hot links for words and phrases that will help you be found in more common searches.

Are you involved in any non-profits, or do you support any charitable causes? This is a good place to make note of it. Others will be especially interested in seeing this side of you.

You do NOT need to be a member of a group or association to list it. There should be some level of affiliation in most cases, but it can be just an "I follow this group" to be able to accurately list it in your profile. This is different from being a "member" of a true LINKEDIN GROUP. (See Appendix B.)

Give some thought to anything that might be controversial with respect to your target audience on LinkedIn. The National Rifle Association, NRA, is one example where you may have to give it some thought. But, if it makes sense, use it, as it creates online, searchable bonds with other NRA members.

Honors and Awards – sticking out from the crowd

"Fame"
– *David Bowie*

"Special"
– *Garbage*

Are you famous for anything, even in very small circles? Don't we all have our 15 seconds of Fame? If you won an award or were recognized for something, say so. President's clubs, employee of the month or year, #1 at something... you get the idea.

Most people have "Something" that they did that was "Special," something for which they were recognized. No "honors and awards police" will come knocking on your door, but don't lie. If you were the top at this or that at one point, say so. It is NOT required, though, that you list anything in here.

If you have any notable honors or awards, by all means mention them if you think the people you are trying to attract will look favorably upon them. Others may search on that particular search term and you will come up. Be proud of your honors.

This is also a great place to identify Professional Credentials that are related to your job, but not tied to one in particular. For example: certifications. My partner, Lori Ruff (www.LinkedIn.com/in/LoriRuff), actually separates her entries in this section. The first subsection is entitled HONORS AND AWARDS. In that she lists selected awards she has received. She follows this with PROFESSIONAL CERTIFICATIONS, where she lists her professional credentials. If one is a Microsoft Certification, for example, you can even list the classes you took or what you studied to help you achieve this certification. Be sure to pack this section—as most others—with keywords that will help you be found.

Include a year if it is relevant. For Example – President's Club award recipient 2002 and 2003. If it is an industry or company award, you can also list how you qualified for the award, how you were selected, or how many people you were chosen from to receive the designation.

Your Personal Information – share a little or a lot

"Call me"
- *Blondie*

Making yourself most available is what might get you the deal vs. someone else. A phone number, which was "officially" off limits to include in LinkedIn Profiles until 2009, is now a must if you are looking for business opportunities, business contacts, or even a job.

This is the newest and one of the handiest features of the profile since the first iteration of this book was released two years ago. Here is the place that LinkedIn finally allows you to officially put your phone number, instant messaging service, address, birthday, and marital status for your connections to

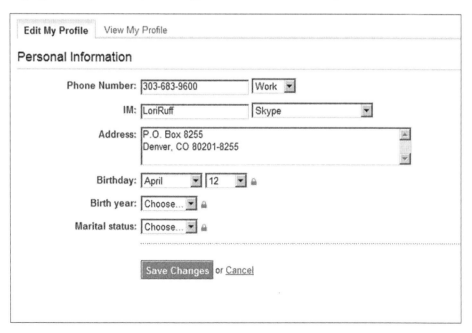

see. Only your first-level connections can see this information, so you may want to duplicate some of this in the Contact Settings section (described next.)

The settings allow you to enter one phone number (home, work or mobile), one instant-messaging service (AIM, Skype, Windows Live Messenger, Yahoo! Messenger, ICQ, or GTalk), your address, birthday, birth year, and marital status. Although I add my full birthday and marital status (simply because I am on the cutting edge, trying everything so you don't have to), the year of your birth and marital status is simply not relevant in most professional settings.

As you enter your information, notice that there is a tiny blue lock beside Birthday, Birth Year, and Marital Status. Just as with your maiden/former name field, this lock allows you to choose whether to show these fields to My Connections (Tier 1 connections only), My Network (Tier 1,2, and 3 connections) or to Everyone (all 50+ million people on LinkedIn).

Contact Settings – how to be reached, who should make contact

"I can't go for that"
– *Hall and Oates*

"Stayin' alive"
– *The Bee Gees*

Different people use LinkedIn differently; it isn't always obvious what is OK and what is not OK in many cases, especially in the world of contacting. If you have any "I can't go for that" restrictions, this is where you should tell people about it. This will most often be the "best way to reach me" vs. the "don't contact me for that." I suggest that you "stay alive" by keeping all the options open and here you have 8 options. How many would you think I suggest you check off? How about Eight Is Enough?

If there are restrictions that you want to put on your availability to be contacted, then this is where it goes. The field entitled "What advice would you give to users considering contacting you?" used to be the unofficial place to put a phone number until LinkedIn came out with a specific section called Personal Information.

Why take cards off the table? Keep all your options open and available by checking all the boxes in the "Opportunity Preferences" section on this screen. You appear approachable and encourage a positive "What's the best way for me to contact this user?" thought, rather than causing the reader to consider the opposite, more negative question "Why doesn't this user want to be contacted?"

LinkedIn gives you some control over a number of aspects of how others may contact you. In fact, you might say that they are mighty generous and thorough with all the options they provide you in the area of being contacted. Since most people are on LinkedIn to

actually use the system and to BE FOUND, the answers to almost all of these options is to select the most "open" options. Let me explain.

First, there are two places to change this information – Contact Settings at the bottom of the "Edit My Profile" screen or in Account and Settings, accessible from the "Settings" link at the top of your page on the right. (Once there, look under the left column Email Notifications.) This configuration area will let you decide which ways or reasons it is OK for others to contact you.

What types of messages will you accept?

I recommend that you select the first option: "I'll accept Introductions, InMail and OpenLink messages." Even if you are trying to build a tight, targeted network consisting of only your peers, you don't want to take away an opportunity for someone you would really want to meet to reach you. If you are a paid subscriber, select the related option to "Include me in the OpenLink Network."

What kinds of opportunities would you like to receive?

- ❏ Career opportunities
- ❏ Consulting offers
- ❏ New ventures
- ❏ Job inquiries

- ❏ Expertise requests
- ❏ Business deals
- ❏ Personal reference requests
- ❏ Requests to connect

I suggest that you always check them all. Unchecked boxes put doubts in people's minds. If they are impressed with your profile and see that you do not have all options available, they may wonder why you don't want to be contacted instead of considering "What's the best way to reach out to Mike so he will want to do business with me?" I hope you see the difference here. The point is to make visiting your profile a positive experience and to remove any barriers of entry to doing business with you. You spend so much time building your profile, being findable, being found, you do not want to do anything to put barriers back in place.

The Contact Settings lets you put in a sizeable amount of text. If there are certain things that someone should know about contacting you, this is the place to put them. Some people include their phone numbers here. Others put in days of the week or times of the day to be contacted. Some put in an email address so anybody can contact them directly via Email rather than having to go through the formal introduction process.

While it is generally not a problem providing this information on LinkedIn, and it does provide a real value for others that may have opportunities for you, there is always a risk in doing so. Only a fraction of the users on LinkedIn put phone numbers and email address in this section of their profiles. Power users usually do. Keep in mind that users must be logged into LinkedIn in order to see this information. Even if you make all of your profile "Public," no one can see Contact Settings until they log into the system.

You need not worry much about privacy here, although it is possible that your information could be "harvested" for bad reasons. This just doesn't seem to happen in the LinkedIn world. The biggest reason is that it is not easy to do it. When you have to look at each user, scroll to the bottom of the screen to see if the information was entered and then copy and paste the information into another program... you get the idea.

The advice you provide should be when and how and why users should contact you. If you are an open networker, here is where you can say you are open to all invitations. If you are an executive seeking to connect only with your peers, say so. People reading your profile who do not recognize themselves as such, are less likely to reach out to you. Phrasing here is critical to opening and closing doors in a positive yet appropriate and professional manner.

Viewing Your Own Profile –
see exactly what others see

"The Man in the Mirror"
– Michael Jackson

It is a best practice to craft your Profile in components, section by section, optimizing it as you go. This allows you to concentrate on the elements that eventually roll up into a finished product. Periodically, it helps to see the big picture, the complete layout.

Look at "the man in the mirror" and see how the whole profile looks when put together. You might even print it out. I like to do this and walk around the house speaking it out loud so I really see what I look like (sound like) to others. If it doesn't read right out loud, change it. You will find a handy printer icon to the right of your picture at the top of your profile.

It is a very good idea to put yourself in the place of your viewer. After all, you create a Profile for OTHERS to find and read about you, don't you? Things look a little different from another user's perspective. This is kind of like looking at Print Preview. This view is particularly useful to see how your use of ALL CAPS, punctuation, and bullets looks to others. Look at it and improve your profile accordingly.

LinkedIn features a tab, View My Profile, just to the right of Edit My Profile for this exact purpose. You can see how others out there see you with all the word wrapping and formatting properly in place.

You should also type your LinkedIn Public Profile URL into an Internet browser address bar to see how your profile looks to people outside of LinkedIn and to check "Your Public Profile" settings. Remember that you can find your Public Profile URL as the last item in the Header section under Websites.

The following screen shot show multiple options to click for the "Edit" or "View" your profile features.

Updating Your Own Profile – staying on top of things

When you keep your LinkedIn profile up-to-date, it shows others that you are engaged and "in the game." Other will "Hear" about your updates through the LinkedIn "Grapevine" called Network Updates. It might prompt them to take a closer look at you.

As you see more and more of other people's profiles, you will get more and more ideas about what you can adopt for use in YOUR profile. A keyword, an adjective, some special characters, or something else that attracted YOU to THEM might attract OTHERS to YOU. No one person or place has all of the ideas nor do they have all the creativity. Early on, in creating your presence on LinkedIn, learn all you can from as many sources as you can find, look at as many profiles as you can, make lots of notes, and then compile the best of them for use in YOUR LinkedIn profile.

Tip! *I suggest that you batch up these updates on a single sheet of paper or in a file and make weekly (or at least monthly) profile changes or tweaks. Of course, you should make them in a word processor and then copy/paste them into your profile.*

Each time you make these updates, others will see that you have something new going on, and you will once again rise to the top of their mind, at least to the top of some of their minds.

It is much the same as with music. Even though we may have our favorite artists, we like the variety more than anything. We may love Michael Jackson's or U2's music, but we don't usually want to listen all day to a radio channel devoted entirely to any one artist, do we? For me, it is a rock channel, perhaps even classic rock, but it is a variety.

LinkedIn Account and Settings – your LinkedIn dashboard

"Welcome to the machine"
— *Pink Floyd*

This is the intensive mechanical (on/off) area of LinkedIn. While there are over a hundred options, we will show you some of the best practices and discuss what the tradeoffs are. This section can have a dramatic impact on your email inbox.

LinkedIn lets you choose a considerable amount of customization of your account settings. They make it very simple by placing most of these settings on a single screen. It is called Account and Settings and can be accessed from the "Settings" link on the upper right hand corner of any screen.

This is similar to the Preferences or Options sections in many applications, especially those from Microsoft and with most browsers.

There are some minor differences between what free users and paid subscribers see, but for the most part it is the same. The only real differences on this screen for free and for paid subscribers will be at the top, where the system shows paid users' remaining balance of InMails and their OpenLink settings.

Let's walk through the Account and Settings screen, section by section, option by option, and discuss what is important in each Subsection. The options will be presented along with recommendations where appropriate. We'll start with the Account area at the top and go down the left side of Settings options. They will explore the right, which you will see is similar to a multi-column newspaper article.

Linked in.   Home   Profile   Contacts   Groups   Jobs   Inbox (1)   More...   Search People ▾

Account

You have a **Business** account. Billing frequency: Annual, Payment method: Visa [Change]
Account Overview | View purchase history | Compare account types

User since July 14, 2005

Get more when you upgrade
✓ **More Communication Features and Access**   ✓ **More Powerful Search**

Upgrade

Introductions: 5 of 15 available
Tip: If your Introductions run out, either wait for a
recipient to take action or upgrade your account.

InMails: 16 available (3 per month)
[Purchase]
InMail Feedback score: ★★★★☆
Your next InMail grant will be on December 9,
2009.

OpenLink Messages: Yes [Change]
As a premium subscriber, you can get OpenLink
messages from any LinkedIn user at no cost to
them.

OpenLink Network: Yes [Change]
Join the OpenLink Network to find other
professionals interested in building new
relationships.

Settings

Profile Settings

My Profile
Update career and education, add associations and awards,
and list specialties and interests.

My Profile Photo
Your profile photo is visible to **everyone.**

Public Profile
Your public profile displays **full profile information.**
http://www.linkedin.com/in/loriruff

Manage Recommendations
You have received 51 recommendations
3 reports, 7 co-workers, 16 clients, 22 partners

Status Visibility
Your current status is visible to **everyone.**

Member Feed Visibility
Your member feed is visible to **everyone.**

Twitter Settings
Add your Twitter account on your profile.

Email Notifications

Contact Settings
You are receiving **Introductions, InMails, and OpenLink
Messages.**

Receiving Messages
Control how you receive emails and notifications.

Invitation Filtering
You are receiving **all invitations.**

Home Page Settings

Network Updates
Settings for the display of Network Updates on your home page.

RSS Settings

Your Private RSS Feeds
Enable or disable your private RSS feeds.

Groups

Group Invitation Filtering
You are **not receiving** Groups Invitations.

My Groups
Settings for groups you manage or belong to.

Groups Order and Display
Set which groups display and in what order in the navigation on
the left side of the page.

Personal Information

Name & Location
Control your name, location, display name, and account holder
icon display settings.

Email Addresses
Your primary email address is currently:
lruff@integratedalliances.com

Change Password
Change your LinkedIn account password.

Close Your Account
Disable your account and remove your profile.

Privacy Settings

Research Surveys
Settings for receiving requests to participate in market research
surveys related to your professional expertise.

Connections Browse
Your connections are **allowed** to view your connections list.

Profile Views
Control what (if anything) is shown to LinkedIn users whose
profile you have viewed.

Viewing Profile Photos
You can view **everyone's** profile photos.

Profile and Status Updates
Control whether your connections are notified when you update
your status or make significant changes to your profile and
whether those changes appear on your company's profile.

Service Provider Directory
If you are recommended as a service provider, you **will** be
listed.

NYTimes.com Customization
Control the LinkedIn-integrated headline customization and
enhanced advertising on NYTimes.com.

Partner Advertising
Control whether you will be shown LinkedIn Audience Network
advertisements on partner websites.

Authorized Applications
See a list of websites or applications you have granted access
to your account and control that access.

My Network

Using Your Network
Tell us how you want to use your LinkedIn network.

Customer Service | About | Blog | Careers | Advertising | Recruiting Solutions | Research Surveys | Tools | Developers | Language | Upgrade Your Account

Use of this site is subject to express terms of use, which prohibit commercial use of this site. By continuing past this page, you agree to abide by these terms.

LinkedIn Corporation © 2009 | User Agreement | Privacy Policy | Copyright Policy | Send us your feedback.

Profile Settings – all in one convenient place

The links here take you to the same place you would go to from the "Edit My Profile" screen where you select "edit" beside each feature. But there are additional settings here as well. So let's go through them all.

My Profile

Just as the Edit my Profile text link on the navigation panel or tab will let you do, so will the "My Profile section" in the Account and Settings screen.

My Profile Photo

This will take you directly to the picture component of your profile. LinkedIn lets you upload a large size picture (4Mb) so you don't have to do any pre-editing. Nice! Upon uploading the picture, you will crop it to an 80x80 pixel SQUARE that is more in the neighborhood of 4kb. You can zoom and pan as one might expect.

Many people think that a highly professional head shot is very important here. Sure, it is a good idea. At 80x80 pixels, however, the cost, time and complexity may be outweighed. A simple photo, even from a high quality camera phone, is usually just fine. Use a simple background (white is best) and a business-like pose and you are off to a great start.

Never do the following:

- Use a logo – it is forbidden by LinkedIn

- Use a picture with more than one person in it – just you and just your head

- Doctor the photo like a cartoon or one of those Obama four-color photos. I know this first-hand as my super-cool "Obamicon" image (shown here) was deleted by LinkedIn.

You have some interesting visibility options. You can limit your photo to be seen only by your direct connections, by those in your network (tiers 1, 2, groups and tier 3), or by everyone. I strongly suggest the last option – everyone. If your name is Pat (or even Chris,) this is especiallyimportant. Can you SEE why?

Public Profile

This section shows you the (assigned or custom) URL to your LinkedIn profile and what sections you want others to see. It is a bit like some of the Account and Settings functions where you have a dashboard enabling you to turn things on and off. I suggest that you have all the sections turned on. After all, that is why you put data into LinkedIn in the first place, isn't it?

Your Public Profile URL is found in your Header area as pictured here.

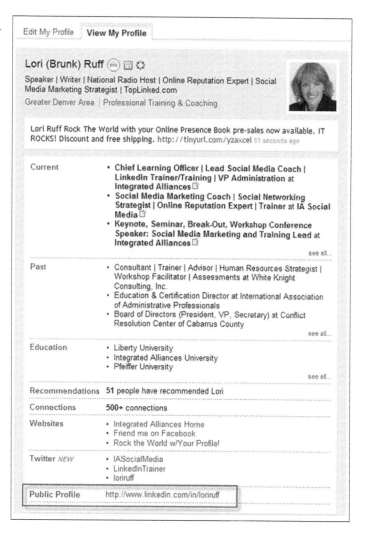

This will give you an idea of where other items in your Account and Settings are reflected.

Manage Recommendations

This section shows you how many recommendations you have and what experience or education listing they are associated with. The Link takes you to the same place you would go to from the Recommendations link on the Profile tab.

There are three tabs available on this screen: Received, Sent, and Request-Recommendations. Watch for tiny links like (Looking for recommendations you've made? Click here.) These will take you to the appropriate screen, but you can also arrive at the same place using the tabs.

Recommendations are addressed in detail in Chapter 5 (Work Experience and Education).

Status Visibility

When you update your status, this section allows you to choose whom it is visible to: My Connections, My Network, or Everyone. Your status appears below your name, headline, and location. It can be edited from the Edit My Profile tab, or from your LinkedIn Home Page.

Member Feed Visibility

"Your personal feed displays Network Updates from actions you have performed on LinkedIn."[4] In everyday language, this means that when you add new connections or join groups, answer questions, or post polls, your activity can be displayed to Nobody, My Connections, My Network or Everyone. Your choice here is dictated by how visible you want to be. Remember that your profile is meant to attract your target market; the more visibility you have, the more likely you are to be noticed.

Tip! *If you want to remain "top of mind" you need to be active in this space. Be careful though not to get sucked in to too much time spent in any one area. Work in batch mode, either daily, a couple of times a week or weekly to actively reach out to connections and to start conversations. Even if that is not a person who needs what you have, they may know someone who does. And, they are much more likely to refer people they know (like you) than someone they don't.*

Twitter Settings

You are now able to connect your LinkedIn Status to Twitter and to multiple Twitter accounts. In addition to adding and removing your Twitter accounts, you can select which account you want to be the primary Twitter account that feeds status updates to your LinkedIn profile. For example, my partner Lori Ruff has three Twitter IDs associated with her LinkedIn profile. She uses @LoriRuff for personal tweeting, @LinkedInTrainer for business

---

[4] *http://www.LinkedIn.com: this statement is found in account and settings/member feed visibility.*

and LinkedIn training in particular, and we both use @iasocialmedia for business in general.

LinkedIn provides two options – 1) share all tweets (I do not recommend this), or 2) share only tweets that contain #in (read as "hashtag in"). Lori has attached @LinkedInTrainer as the primary Twitter account on her LinkedIn profile so that every time she tweets in accordance with the second option, Twitter updates her LinkedIn status.

One important note here: Where there are multiple people updating the same Twitter account (i.e., a company account), everyone with access can associate the Twitter account to their individual LinkedIn accounts. For example, the Twitter handle @iasocialmedia is our company account. Fellow executive Lori Ruff and I both have access on Twitter. We both have connected this Twitter ID to our LinkedIn accounts, so that as when we update our LinkedIn status concerning company rather than personal projects, we both also have the option to update the company account on Twitter.

As I said when discussing Network Status Updates, the importance of the integration between LinkedIn and Twitter cannot be overstated. The brilliance of this feature is your ability to selectively and strategically coordinate status communications between your LinkedIn and Twitter "networks" in either one or both directions (from LinkedIn to Twitter and/or Twitter to LinkedIn).

For more details about the Twitter application, see Chapter 3 (Your Status) and Chapter 9 (LinkedIn Applications).

Email Notifications — what comes to you and what doesn't

"Message in a bottle"
– The Police

"Don't you want me, baby"
– Human League

While it may seem like there are a lot of messages and emails "floating around out there," the email configuration capabilities in LinkedIn can get that under control rather quickly.

LinkedIn lets you get quite granular with what comes in to you through actual email's to your email inbox. The other options are to receive your communications through the equivalent of "webmail," where you go to LinkedIn itself to see and answer your communications or to shut yourself off almost entirely from receiving communications (not recommended).

Contact Settings

This section shows configured settings in the Profile Contact Settings section. The link takes you to the Edit Contact Settings Section of your Profile discussed earlier in this book.

Receiving Messages

Deciding which communications come to you via email will be a process and not a one-time thing. Try different options and see what works best for you. For example, InMails and Introductions are more timely and, therefore, of greater importance for coming through in emails than invitations.

This section has a lot of interesting settings that you can configure. The illustration shows the screen. Following this are explanations of the options, along with specific strategies to consider. When you move your mouse over the question-mark icon you see on the screen, a pop-up box tells you a bit about each of the options.

It is important when considering how you want to receive messages to understand that each of the messages you receive always arrives in your Inbox on LinkedIn. If you also choose to receive individual email or daily or weekly digests (where applicable). Then you will also receive the message in your email Inbox. That means that you have to deal with the message twice. And, if you are not careful, you may even answer it twice: once from your email Inbox and once from your LinkedIn Inbox!

InMails, Introductions and OpenLink – You usually want to get these right away. They represent opportunities and requests by people to be passed through to you to connect. If you choose Web Only (versus Individual emails or Weekly Digest), you can reduce the clutter in your Inbox. However, you should be diligent and look daily at LinkedIn if you elect the Web Only option. These are important communications that you may miss and you may negatively affect the lives of others and your own reputation if you don't check it daily. People depend on your prompt response. Here is a great way to be a Giver in this Pay-It-Forward community.

Receiving Messages

LinkedIn will send you a notification when you receive important messages from other users. How would you like to receive these notifications?

	Individual Email (Send emails to me immediately)	Daily Digest Email (Send one bundle per day)	Weekly Digest Email (Send one bundle email per week)	No Email (Read messages on the website)
General				
InMails, Introductions, and OpenLink	●	Not Available	○	○
Invitations	○	Not Available	○	●
Profile Forwards	○	Not Available	○	●
Job Notifications	○	Not Available	○	●
Questions from your Connections	○	Not Available	○	●
Replies/Messages from connections	●	Not Available	○	○
Messages between pending group applicants and group managers	○	Not Available	●	○
Network Updates	Not Available	Not Available	○	●
Discussions				
Network Update Activity	○	Not Available	Not Available	●
Groups				
Invitations to join groups	○	Not Available	○	●
Group Digest Emails				
48 HOURS OPEN NETWORKING (We Accept all invites within 48 hours)	Not Available	○	○	●
500+	Not Available	○	○	●
CEO/ CIO/COE/COO/CFO/Head/VP/ Director/President Level - Senior Leadership Group	Not Available	○	○	●

The Digest email is really only for very casual users. I suggest you select the Individual email or Web Only options. Personally, I do all my administration on the Web, so I select the last option. Unless otherwise specified, the same overall strategies apply for all of the options below as well.

Invitations – People will send you invitations to connect with them on LinkedIn. When you accept, you become Tier 1 Connections and have more opportunities to find resources and expand your search results. Like the options above, these messages can be sent one at a time, in a weekly digest, or via the web only.

Profile Forwards – Other people have the ability to turn you onto someone that they think will be a good connection for you. One way they can do this is through Profile Forwards. Like the others above, they can be sent one at a time, in a weekly digest, or via the web only.

Good etiquette in this community indicates that you should not only view the profile, but you should reply to those who sent them and let them know if they are a good fit. That will help them help you again in the future, and it allows you to thank them for thinking about you.

Job Notifications – This is when your connections forward you job opportunities to you. It is a notification of jobs for you or someone you know. Recruiters will often use this feature to promote positions that they have available. They are seldom directed specifically to you, so I suggest that you pick the Web Only option here if you are not actively searching for a position. If you are, ask your connections to keep an eye out for you and to forward any postings they find that might be applicable.

Questions from your Connections – This is a tie-in with the LinkedIn Answers blog-type capability. It can be a bit bothersome as most of the questions have nothing to do with you. I suggest the Web Only option here as well.

Replies/Messages from Connections – These are replies to your outbound communications to others. I suggest that you select the Individual Email option here unless you work in batch mode, daily checking your LinkedIn InBox.

Network Updates – This is heavily composed of information of very little value for most people. It consists of changes your contacts have made to their profiles or their networks and their activity on LinkedIn. You can also show Network updates on your LinkedIn Home Page, where the information is more easily filtered and addressed. For the most part, though, the email version is very distracting, so I suggest that you select the Web Only option here.

Messages between Pending Group Applicants and Group Managers –If you operate or manage a LinkedIn Group, this will send messages to your Inbox when people send a message "to the Group Manager," for example, with requests to join. Unless you check your Group every day, I recommend individual or weekly digest emails. Weekly digest works well here, because it allows you to work in batch mode and sends you a reminder to check pending group messages. It is important to accept requests to join quickly, so as to allow people to become engaged when they are interested.

Discussions – Status Activity – Unlike Network Activity, this is composed of updates about your connections' Status Updates when you have participated in a discussion. I don't participate in these discussions; my network is so large, it would become cumbersome. However, one of my team does comment on her connections status when it intrigues her. Often they will reply, and she receives that message to her email so she can promptly reply and keep the conversation going. She has connected with some very interesting people using this strategy.

Groups – This is a listing of every LinkedIn group you belong to. If the group is your own, if it is work-related, or if you are interested in the discussion or new to the group, you may want to select the Daily or Weekly Digest. However, it can be distracting, so I suggest that you select the Web Only option here for most groups.

And at the very bottom of the screen – LinkedIn gives you the option to receive messages about new features and tips. They come about once a month, and it is a good idea to receive them. We suggest you keep this box checked.

Invitation Filtering

This section tells you how your invitation filtering is set. Business professionals, job seekers, etc. should select All Invitations. If you are a busy executive without a Managed Services team or administrative team to back you up, you may want to select the second option to be notified of Invitations only when someone knows your email address or is in your Imported Contacts list. This reduces the number of invitations you receive while still making it easy for people who know you to connect with you.

The final option: "Only invitations from people who appear in my 'Imported Contacts' list" should be used with care. LinkedIn includes this "Tip:

Don't miss invitations from people who matter to you. Add people to your 'Imported Contacts' list." The point is, if you do not have them in your Imported contact list, ready to send them an invitation, even if they know your email address, they cannot SEND you an invitation to connect. By selecting the second option, you can reduce the number of invitations you receive, but you still have the option to accept or at least receive those from people who are more likely to know you personally.

Home Page Settings – what do you want to see or NOT see?

"**Walk this way**"
Aerosmith

"**All I want to do**"
Sheryl Crow

Customizing your Home Page settings lets you walk the way that is just the right way for you. Aerosmith walks their way, don't they? There are all kinds of options that allow you to make LinkedIn work just the way you want it. When you log into LinkedIn, you are brought to your customized Home Page.

Some people may want to do it all, turn it all on. Others may be the more "all I want to do" types. I am somewhere in the middle, while my partner, Lori Ruff turns on as much as possible to stay more engaged with her network. She uses the Network Updates like an interactive newspaper.

Network Updates

This link takes you to a screen where you determine which network updates you want to appear on your Home Page. This is very similar to the Network Updates that you would receive via email if you chose to receive them. The page opens to the "Manage Updates by Connections" tab. Click on "Manage Updates by Type" to access these options.

Select to checkbox to "Hide Network Updates" if you want to clean up your Home Page. If you want to show any, you can also select how many (from 10, 15, 20 or 25) to show.

This can be a great tool to help you start conversations and reach out to connections with whom you find you have interests in common. You can congratulate people who update their profiles with new positions that might represent new customers for you; comment on someone's status if you find it intriguing; comment on questions or answers from your connections; see new jobs, events or polls posted by your connections; be notified of new groups your connections joined (giving you ideas on groups you may want to consider), see new application updates (if someone updates their **Amazon. com** reading list or SlideShare); or see new or updated Company Profiles from your connections (this could provide ideas for new customers or expanding your existing customer base).

RSS Feeds – a great way to stay in touch

If you are familiar with RSS (Real Syndication Service) feeds, this is where you can enable the feed to your favorite reader or by an RSS link for Network Updates and/or LinkedIn Answers.

Here is what LinkedIn has to say:

> "RSS is a technology that gives you access to LinkedIn content through your favorite RSS feed reader. LinkedIn offers two types of feeds, public and personal. Public feeds offer the same content to all LinkedIn members. Personal feeds contain private information from your LinkedIn network."

LinkedIn Groups – places to meet, interact with others

"Run with the pack"
– Bad Company

Getting involved with LinkedIn Groups greatly increases your circle of contacts and influence. Members of the same "pack" can join in group discussions and even send messages to one another, like fellow fan club members might do.

LinkedIn Groups are all the rage and for good reason. People are on LinkedIn to meet and interact with others with whom they can establish valuable business relationships. When those others are more highly qualified, or when they share common interests with you, it is even better.

LinkedIn Groups do just that – they let you self-associate with others who have similar interests, and they provide tools for collaboration with fellow group members. Groups have become so important in the LinkedIn world that we have devoted an entire section specifically to this area (Appendix B).

Group Invitation Filtering

Here is where you can indicate if you are interested in receiving Group Invitations. In today's environment, there are about half a million groups, and more are being added each day. Now, that number may seem overwhelming, but if you search on a topic you are interested in and join the largest of the groups meeting your target, you should be in good shape. If you leave this feature on, make sure you couple it with your email Notifications: Receiving Messages: Groups: Invitations to Join Groups: No email. Otherwise, this feature can become overwhelming and might discourage you from taking full advantage of everything this powerful tool has to offer you.

My Groups – people interested in the same things as you

"We belong"
– *Pat Benatar*

"Nobody's fault but mine"
– *Led Zeppelin*

LinkedIn Groups give you a sense of belonging, sort of like a fan club in the real world. People that attend the same concerts tend to have other things in common too, don't they? Don't Pink Floyd or Grateful Dead fans tend to get along well with one another?

A search of LinkedIn Groups for "Band OR Music" brings up 2,500+ results! The keywords "Grateful Dead" brings up seven groups. In a way, LinkedIn Groups is where you rub elbows with your peers, people you share fun interests with, and even Social Media Rock Stars.

If you don't get enough out of LinkedIn and you haven't participated in LinkedIn Groups – whose fault is it? Zep folks know the power of groups; isn't it time you dove in as well?

Since you can join up to 50 LinkedIn Groups (and now 50 subgroups as well), you should probably belong to at least 20-30 groups. I always try to keep a few available slots (I belong to about 45 at any one time) so I can join groups that I run across daily in traveling through the profiles of others.

You can order the way LinkedIn Groups appear on your profile. List the most important or your favorites on top. Why have it be a random order? If you don't particularly like the order, whose fault is that now that you know you have the power to arrange them the way you want? Keep in min444444ed that the order is only affected on your own profile. The way other people see your list may still show up randomly, depending on LinkedIn's functionality at the time.

The My Groups link takes you to your LinkedIn Groups page, which is also available from the navigation menu. It allows you to change settings for the groups you manage and for those to which you belong. For each Group in the list, click on "Settings" under the name of the Group to make adjustments. The options include Visibility Settings, Contact Settings, and Updates Settings. Again, these choices will be determined by how much communication you want to receive from each group.

Groups Order and Display

Here is where you can change the order that your Groups display on you, My Groups, as well as how many and in what order they show up on your navigation menu. You can show from one to ten on the menu. There are links on the right of each Group name that gives you easy access to Manager and Member settings. Remember that this includes Visibility, Contact, and Updates settings.

The Contact Settings allows you to select one of your alternate email addresses to receive communications from the Group, so if you have a personal interest group, but your main email is your work address, here is where you can have the messages for this group go to a personal email address instead.

Remember to check where your group messages go if you discontinue using a work or personal email. If you do not do this, a perpetual message "One or more of your email addresses have bounced" will appear across the top of your home page. Without access to reconfirm the email, you won't be able to get rid of the message without help from LinkedIn.

Personal Information – how to reach you

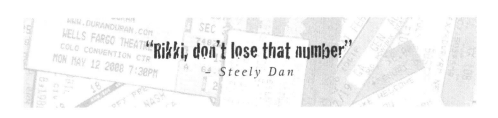

"Rikki, don't lose that number"
— *Steely Dan*

LinkedIn used to be much more secretive of you and your contact information. You could not include a phone number, address, or email address without technically violating their end user license agreement. Now it is considered a best practice, an acceptable way to make doing business easier, and there are even dedicated fields and a proper way to do it. With the addition of tags and new contact features being tested and implemented regularly, LinkedIn is much more like an online database for many, me included. I never "lose that number" when my connections put it in their LinkedIn Profile.

Name & Location

This sounds simple and it really is. Put in your First Name, your Last Name, Zip Code where you work or live. We suggest that you use a work ZIP code here. Why is this important? The ZIP Code becomes the default ZIP code for searches where you choose the Location option.

Display Name: While you CAN choose to show others only your First Name and Last Initial, DO NOT DO THIS unless you want to make your name private to people outside of your network. If you choose this option, people who are Tier 1 connections will see your full name; everyone else in your network will see your first name and last initial. People not in your network will only see generic information, such as your title and company. Simply go with First Name and Last Name in your display.

NOTE: This screen only allows you to change/update your first and last name; whereas, if you go to Edit Your Profile and click on "edit" beside your name, you also have the option described earlier to add/change/update your maiden/former name.

If you choose to add anything else to your name, such as MBA, Ph.D or "My Specialty," add it AFTER your last name in the last name field so that you can still be found where people would expect to find you when they look for you in an alphabetic listing. LinkedIn has recently updated its indexing features to enhance the findability of name fields. However, some people take this too far and use questionable strategies.

The following strategies are frowned upon by LinkedIn (and many users) and should be avoided. We have heard of people whose profiles have been terminated for violating this rule (found in the End User License Agreement, or EULA). For example:

1. Some people put their email address in the Last name field. LinkedIn specifically prohibits this (fields are to be used only for their intended purpose). It is a bad practice; don't do it. You can accomplish the increased visibility for your email address by putting it in your Headline or at the top of your Summary.

2. Some people use special characters (like !, ., or #) as the first character in their last name. Why? Many search engines sort the results of searches alphabetically. People believe special characters like these appear first in the display of searches. These people are trying to "beat the system" and get themselves to appear first in listings. DO NOT DO THIS. It actually backfires. If you look at your Contacts page, you will see A – Z listed, followed by #. This is where LinkedIn puts profiles when the last name field begins with special characters. They don't show up first. And it makes it hard for people to find you. It may seem like the right thing to do, but it is not.

Account Holder Icon – If you are a paid subscriber, this screen will also allow you to select whether or not you want to display the little gold "IN" box beside your name on your profile. This indicates to people that you have upgraded your account to a paid account. I suggest that you always display it because it makes you stand out, and look special, and it adds to your credibility as a professional that takes full advantage of the tools available for success.

Paid Business Accounts – LinkedIn has expenses to cover to offer this great service. One of the ways they make ends meet is to have a premium service

– Paid Business Accounts. The premium levels of service start at $24.95/mo. Pay for a year up front and get two months free.

While the features change from time to time, usually with more being added, they include the following:

Introductions – LinkedIn provides five with a free account. A basic upgrade to a Paid Business Account gets you 15 instead.

InMails – With a free account, LinkedIn does not provide InMails. A basic upgrade to a Paid Business Account gets you three per month. They roll over a bit and accumulate in your account.

Search Results – Free account holders see up to 300 results when they search. Basic Paid Business Account holders get 500 instead; higher-level premium accounts get even more.

OpenLink Messages – LinkedIn users have lots of ways to communicate with one another. OpenLink is one of these methods that is only available to Paid Business Account holders. However, they are not widely used in the LinkedIn world. When a paid subscriber elects to receive OpenLink messages, other users can send a free InMail message to the subscriber.

Account Holder Icon – LinkedIn will place, at your option, a nifty gold icon on your profile showing others that you are a Paid Business Account Holder. This shows that you are a serious LinkedIn user, and it gets you extra attention in the LinkedIn community. This is like a shiny object that attracts people's attention and gets them clicking on YOUR profile instead of someone else's. It does for me!

Profile Organizer – LinkedIn's Profile Organizer feature lets you "tag" other users with attributes, placing them in folders. This bookmarks their profiles for quick retrieval at a later date. You can also add up to 1000 characters of notes and additional contact information. When you export your contact list, this information is exported as well, helping you differentiate between connections and solid contacts. The Basic Paid Business Account gives you five such folders to organize profiles.

So, $24.95 gets you started with a Basic Paid Business Account. Pay more for a Business Plus account ($49.95/mo) or a Pro Account ($499.95/mo) and receive a larger quantity of the above. More money does not get you more features, just larger quantities of these enticing features.

This is a very important area of LinkedIn. This section of the Account and Settings screen shows which Email address is your "primary" Email address. If you have only one email address associated with your profile then this is simple.

LinkedIn lets you assign multiple email addresses to your LinkedIn Profile. YOU WANT TO PUT ALL OF YOUR ACTIVE EMAIL ADDRESSES IN YOUR LINKEDIN PROFILE HERE AND YOU WANT TO DO IT NOW. Why? Let's go through this scenario. You put in just one email address in your LinkedIn Profile. Someone sends you an invitation to your OTHER email address, the one NOT in your LinkedIn profile. Now what?

1. LinkedIn looks through all of the email addresses in its database.

2. It doesn't find a match, so it assumes this is for a new user.

3. It then sends you an email prompting you to create a NEW profile.

4. Now you are confused at best, and you most likely will create a second profile. Having two profiles is bad, undesirable and a violation of the LinkedIn End User License Agreement. At worst, you don't get the invitation or opportunity to connect because you no longer have access to the old email.

So, avoid this problem by putting in all of your email addresses in your profile now.

This is the process (follow it carefully):

1. At the top of the screen, under "Add Email Address" enter each alternate address and click on the Add Email Address button.

2. The email address then is listed under Current Email Addresses. Down below and beside it, you will see "Unconfirmed." The system will automatically send you a confirmation message.

   a. If you need to resend the confirmation message, click on the radio button to highlight the new email address.

   b. Click then on the Send Confirmation Message button at the bottom. This resends an email to that address that will appear in your email inbox. The email has a link on it that leads you through the confirmation process.

3. Once the email address is confirmed, it will say "Confirmed."

4. Repeat the process for all of your email addresses.

5. Select which one you want to be your "Primary Email Address" by clicking on the radio button and then select the Make Primary button. This is the email address that LinkedIn will use for most communications. It will also appear at the bottom of your LinkedIn profile to your Tier 1 connections.

Tip! *Some people will set-up an email address specifically for their LinkedIn activities. There are a lot of reasons for this, and it is considered to be a best practice by many. It might be a GMAIL, Yahoo or Hotmail email address. I suggest Sales, Marketing and Business Development Professionals use the company email address for branding purposes. This is a business tool, after all.*

Tip! *Do not delete old email addresses because people might try to connect with you through those old accounts. LinkedIn will send email messages to your primary email even if it is sent with the old address, so it is to your benefit to keep them and change your primary email when you change addresses. Imagine all the old business cards that have an old email address on them. Even if people use those old emails to reach out to connect with you on LinkedIn, they will find you if you keep the address associated with your account.*

If you leave a company or close an old email account, just remember to change your primary address. If you selected an address other than your primary account for any group messages, you will need to change those as well. It is a best practice to review you group settings once a month or once a quarter to ensure that you are receiving the messages you want.

Change Password

This is just what it seems ... very straightforward. You will enter it often, so make it simple and memorable. You may want to make it unique for LinkedIn. I recommend that you keep an Excel file where you can track the website, username, and password of all – or most – of your usernames.

Close Your Account

Many people ask how to close their accounts. The system will ask why you want to close the account and ask for verification before it lets you delete your account. This is an important place for people who have multiple Profiles.

If you do have multiple accounts, make sure you invite all your contacts to the profile you want to keep. Copy all of your profile information to a Word document so you have it. Finally, if you have recommendations on one profile and not the other, even if the one without recommendations has more connections, close the one without the recommendations as they are more difficult to replace.

Privacy Settings - never be too careful nor too available

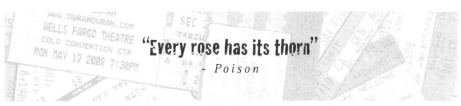

"Every rose has its thorn"
- *Poison*

Remember the physics principle that every action has an opposite and equal reaction? There are indeed tradeoffs (pros and cons) to consider when you expose yourself in the public eye. It is happening, whether you like it or not, and LinkedIn at least lets you reel it in if you feel that it has gone too far. Having a presence on LinkedIn lets you control your credibility.

Research Surveys

This Subsection has "Settings" for receiving requests to participate in market-research surveys related to your professional expertise. This is LinkedIn's official statement:

> "LinkedIn and its research partners may invite a select group of users to participate in online market research studies. Users are identified based on non-personal information such as job title, company size, or region. Participation is 100 percent voluntary, and personal information such as name and email address will never be revealed."

There is not much more to say here other than to let you know that in the years I have been a LinkedIn user, I do not remember receiving any requests to participate in such a survey. If they use this feature—and I am sure they do—then it is likely to be infrequent so as not to impose on members' time. With 50 million-plus members and more coming on every day, there is ample opportunity to get a large enough sample size without asking everyone, or even any one person very often, for participation.

Connections Browse

This is an important setting. LinkedIn lets you choose if you want your Tier 1 connections to be able to directly see who your other Tier 1 connections are. There are times and places where it makes sense to hide your connections (executives and recruiters with small networks, for example), but most business professionals are not usually part of this group. Again, it implies a negative question: "What is he/she trying to hide?" instead of the person reading your Profile asking "What is the best method for me to reach out to this user so that they will want to do business with me?"

I suggest that you leave Connections Browsing enabled. Those who hide their connections are frowned upon in the LinkedIn community, as they seem to be "takers" and not "givers." It defeats much of the purpose of online networking. Even with it turned off, others can still search your network and find your direct (and Tier 2 and Tier 3) connections. They just can't click on this tab and see a listing of your Tier 1 connections displayed. And, if you look at someone's connections, you will see it is not a convenient alphabetical listing that indicates which are your customers or vendors, or which are connections that you might not even know personally. The only indication on your Profile if someone is a client or vendor is when they write a recommendation for you that you have publicly displayed.

Profile Views

This is another important setting. LinkedIn lets you see who views your profile and vice versa. If you look at someone's profile, LinkedIn can tell them a little, a lot, or nothing about your being there. LinkedIn defaults this option to show others anonymous information such as the job title and industry or company (if it is a large company) of users who view their profiles. The other options are to show your name and headline, or to show nothing.

For the most part, I suggest that you do not show anyone that you have visited their Profile. It usually has no advantage to you. Why? If you are conducting business intelligence, you may not want the people you are looking at to know that you are looking at them.

However, some people do show their information, either their anonymous information or their full information. This can be a great setting for job seekers who want recruiters and hiring managers to see that they have done their homework. Recruiters and hiring managers, on the other hand, may not want job seekers to see that they have been doing theirs!

Viewing Profile Photos

Of course you want to see the photos of others. Say Yes to Everyone, unless you are in recruiting or HR.

In fact, LinkedIn includes the ability to turn this feature off just for these individuals. Many Recruiting and HR professionals need to be able to block viewing of photos so they do not get involved in discrimination situations.

This is a good point to note for job seekers who ask "I'm older, should I include my photo?" The answer is yes; show your picture (as long as you can come up with a good one)! Also, it is better to add a good picture taken from a camera phone against a white wall rather than putting off adding a photo until you can get a professional picture made. The resulting picture is only 80x80 pixels!

Profile and Status Updates

LinkedIn can send notifications to your connections when you change your Profile or your Status. When you update your Profile, it will also update the Company Profile if your company has one adding you to the "Movers and Shakers" list. To see this, look at the top of your screen and click on the "More..." link and select "Companies."

If you plan to make several changes to your profile, you may want to turn this feature off for now. But turn it back on when you are done so that when you update your profile in bits and pieces later, it will update the company information and send a notice to your connections through the Profile Update feature. It will also list you on the "Movers and Shakers" list. This is on the Company Profile that lists New Hires, Recent Promotions and Changes, Past Employees, and Popular Profiles.

Service Provider Directory

Of course you want to be listed in the Service Provider Directory. Pick YES. We are here to promote our business and service, after all. Note that you will not be added to the directory until you receive a recommendation as a service provider. If this is important to you, be sure to ask for a recommendation and specify that you'd like to be recommended as a service provider.

Partner Advertising

LinkedIn lets you choose if you want to see random ads or see ads that are more targeted toward your interests. Select the targeted option.

Authorized Applications

If you have allowed applications access to your profile so that you could use the application plug-ins, this is where you can delete their access. There are other plug-ins available under External websites such as the LinkedIn toolbar, the LinkedIn plug-in for Outlook, and perhaps XOBNI (InBox spelled backwards,) an external plug-in for Outlook that accesses information in LinkedIn to enhance your communications with your connections from within Outlook. (www.xobni.com)

Check each of the applications that you want to remove and then click the Remove button at the bottom of the page.

My Network – what are you using it for?

LinkedIn asks why you are on LinkedIn using its network. Even though you may not be interested in all of these reasons, SELECT THEM ALL. Why? You want to be as open as possible to opportunities for you and your company. Remember that people will use LinkedIn in the way that they think makes sense. And LinkedIn will use this information when they determine what enhancements to make. The more enhancements that they make, the better the user experience should become for everyone.

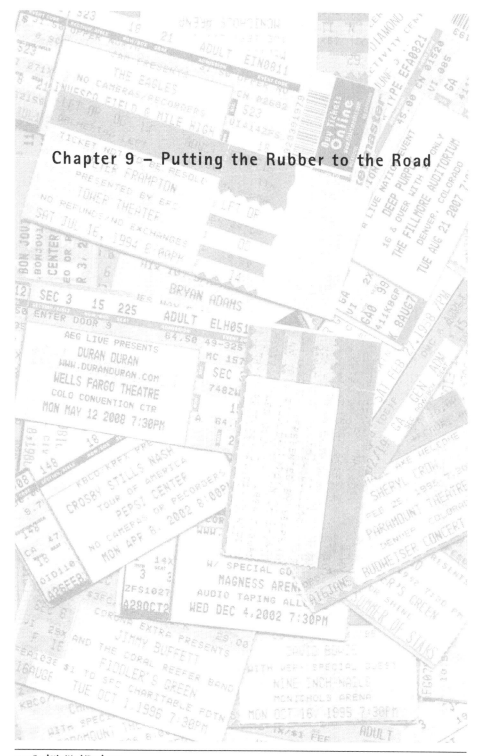

Chapter 9 – Putting the Rubber to the Road

LinkedIn Applications – plug this one in please

We are at the dawn of a whole new era in LinkedIn – Applications. While Facebook has hundreds of thousands of applications that run INSIDE of Facebook, LinkedIn has just a few. There will undoubtedly be more applications added down the road.

The newest craze in LinkedIn is Applications. In late 2008, LinkedIn opened the door to ten carefully selected companies to provide a "plug-in" capability for their applications to reside DIRECTLY INSIDE your LinkedIn account. They have since added 2 more. You can choose to grant the application access to your account so that you can use it and decide if you want to show it on your Home Page, your profile or both.

As opposed to Facebook, where anyone can develop an application to join the 10,000 plus other applications, LinkedIn kept this offering very small and tight. LinkedIn's limited applications actually help in business collaboration, as it is very clear what application will be used for what purpose. This allows each application the opportunity to build a strong following, so it is easy to find consistency between connections. We will touch on these applications at a high level and discuss how they might be used.

Some of the applications have common functions, although each was chosen by LinkedIn for different reasons. None are mutually exclusive at a technical level. For example, WordPress and Blog Link applications overlap in their offerings, but they each have different features as well. The SlideShare and Google Presentation, and Huddle Workspace and Box.net applications also do similar things, but there are reasons a user would select one application over the other, or in some cases, both.

LinkedIn Applications enable you to enrich your profile, share and collaborate with your network, and get the key insights that help you be more effective. Applications are added to your homepage and profile enabling you to control who gets access to what information.

Huddle Workspaces
by Huddle.net

Huddle gives you private, secure online workspaces packed with simple yet powerful project, collaboration and sharing tools for working with your connections.

Google Presentation
by Google

Present yourself and your work. Upload a .PPT or use Google's online application to embed a presentation on your profile.

Blog Link
by SixApart

With **Blog Link**, you can get the most of your LinkedIn relationships by connecting your blog to your LinkedIn profile. Blog Link helps you, and your professional network, stay connected.

SAP Community Bio
by LinkedIn

Display your certified SAP expertise on LinkedIn. The **SAP Community Bio** application allows you to add your SAP contributions and credentials to your professional profile.

SlideShare Presentations
by SlideShare Inc

SlideShare is the best way to share presentations on LinkedIn! You can upload & display your own presentations, check out presentations from your colleagues, and find experts within your network.

Box.net Files
by Box.net

Add the Box.net Files application to manage all your important files online. Box.net lets you share content on your profile, and collaborate with friends and colleagues.

Reading List by Amazon
by Amazon

Extend your professional profile by sharing the books you're reading with other LinkedIn members. Find out what you should be reading by following updates from your connections, people in your field, or other LinkedIn members of professional interest to you.

Tweets
by LinkedIn

Access the most important parts of the professional conversation with Tweets, a Twitter client you can use right on LinkedIn.

WordPress
by WordPress

Connect your virtual lives with the WordPress LinkedIn Application. With the WordPress App, you can sync your WordPress blog posts with your LinkedIn profile, keeping everyone you know in the know.

Company Buzz
by LinkedIn

Ever wonder what people are saying about your company? **Company Buzz** shows you the twitter activity associated with your company. View tweets, trends and top key words. Customize your topics and share with your coworkers.

Events
by LinkedIn

Find professional events, from conferences to local meet-ups, and discover what events your connections are attending.

My Travel
by TripIt, Inc

See where your LinkedIn network is traveling and when you will be in the same city as your colleagues. Share your upcoming trips, current location, and travel stats with your network.

Polls
by LinkedIn

The **Polls** application is a market research tool that allows you to collect actionable data from your connections and the professional audience on LinkedIn.

Applications have a lot of Importance

You can see the importance that LinkedIn places on this new capability based on where the applications are located. LinkedIn puts the applications that you grant access to your profile just below Specialties and above Experience. This is prime real estate from a marketing perspective, being right about where "the fold" might be in a publication.

Expect to see the importance of Applications increase tremendously in the next year, as more and more users figure out how to harness these valuable tools for business. This is the logical result as the number of users increase and they spend more time on LinkedIn.

LinkedIn's Applications appear on your Profile and your LinkedIn Home Page, based on your selection when you grant each one access.

LinkedIn's Applications bring extra attention to your profile and to you. They help you stand out from the crowd, and they provide functionality that can help you personally and in business. This is the benefit of the "public view" of your applications on your profile. Not everybody will use Applications, and certainly not everybody will use ALL of the Applications.

Another place where you may view your applications is from your LinkedIn Home Page. This is the private view of your applications. It is where you will usually go to manage your applications, and where you can test them out before you "turn them on."

Where to shop for and install Applications

This prime real estate was previously occupied by Work Experience so that indicates the importance that LinkedIn gives these new tools.

 Tip! *By default, Applications DO NOT automatically appear on your profile or on your Home Page. You must ENABLE this capability. And, don't worry, if you change your mind, you can remove the application as well.*

You will find applications that you have installed listed on the navigation menu under "More...". By default, nobody has ANY applications installed. Each one must be manually enabled by you. Clicking on the text link Application Directory on your navigation panel will take you to the Applications Preview Page (a landing page) where you can select, install, and configure the applications on your Profile and/or on your Home Page. This landing page highlights the applications, in rotating order. When you click Browse

More Applications on the top right of the applications screen at this point, it just shuffles the order. Eventually, as LinkedIn adds more applications, it will probably lead to some kind of search screen.

How they appear

One can decide whether or not the Applications appear on one's Profile, on the LinkedIn Home Page, or both. There are strategies for each, and we will touch briefly on them here.

The Applications appear in a particular order on a LinkedIn profile, and this order cannot be affected. The order in which they appear on the Navigation Panel does NOT directly correlate to the order in which they appear in one's LinkedIn profile itself.

 Applications show up on your profile in the order in which you grant them access from the top down, so select carefully.

With the exception of its own apps, applications are not specifically designed for LinkedIn. They are SUBSETS of full-blown applications that appear elsewhere on the web. Each has a fully featured big brother that you can use as well. In fact, in many cases, the services provide additional user functionality, if you go to the main site for the application and work with it from there. The plug-ins are designed to be more like a sample to allow you to highlight certain aspects of your business. They don't give you access to a full-blown application environment.

Here is the suite of LinkedIn Applications as of this writing:

LinkedIn Events

 LinkedIn has one of its own applications called Events that gets bundled into the navigation menu. It is functional and helps you promote events to your LinkedIn connections. It also gives you the option to promote or advertise events to other LinkedIn users. However, it is not the easiest application to use.

This product is still in development, and they have a lot of work to do. But if you promote events, you should learn to use this now, so that as upgrades are made, you will be able to incorporate them into your regular routine more easily.

One glitch is that you can't keep past events from showing on your profile, so if you don't have any upcoming events, I recommend that you go into the settings and only show this application on your home page, not your profile. That way you won't come across as looking out-of-date.

SlideShare

This is one of the most popular of the applications that LinkedIn provides access to. The full-blown application can be found at **www.SlideShare.NET** (not .COM). It allows users to upload a presentation in a variety of formats and have those applications appear directly within your LinkedIn profile. SlideShare is rich in functionality, but the advanced features require you to go to the SlideShare site to gain access to the really powerful capabilities. SlideShare also has a plug-in for Facebook, so if you are also on that platform, this is an excellent choice to allow you interaction between your social media sites.

SlideShare supports over ten types of file formats for uploading, so you are sure to get what you need. And with 100Mb of space provided in the freebase package, most people have all the space they need.

LinkedIn does NOT currently support any video file formats. But, by going to directly the SlideShare.Net site, you can add a YouTube video to an existing presentation. As of this writing, only one video can be inserted before the first slide, or after the last slide of the presentation. If you want the video to show on your profile, then you need to insert it before the first slide.

Google Presentation

Surprisingly, the Google Presentation application does not have that awesome Google power that one might expect. It is strictly for sharing presentations. No application sharing, no Google Calendars, nothing fancy. Like the others (e.g. SlideShare, Box, Huddle,) it can share PPTs, PDFs, DOCs and Spreadsheets. However, there is one thing that it does above and beyond all the rest: You can actually CREATE a presentation in your LinkedIn account and insert video within it.

Look for Google to be adding more functionality in this area down the road. It is highly unusual to see limited functionality in ANY Google product. I would not expect it to stay that way for long.

This application is designed mostly for business travelers. It lets you enter your travel schedule with a great level of detail (which requires you to visit the TripIt site directly). LinkedIn can then provide a variety of useful pieces of information. For example it will tell you who else is traveling to the same city at the same time. You can also alert others to your travel plans.

Within TripIt you can add connections and share travel information with them. This is very handy when you want to keep abreast of the itineraries of business associates, or when you want to make plans to meet some of the connections you have made on LinkedIn as you travel to or through their cities. We use this feature when we travel to connect in person with people who might help us get business done.

You have several interesting options for inputting data into TripIt:

- Forward your travel confirmations directly to TripIt (plans@tripit. com) and they will automatically parse out the data and upload it into your account.

- Manually enter the destination, location, dates, and a description of your trip for others to see.

- You can choose to hide trips or share them with your connections.

The TripIt summary screen is like a dashboard that shows upcoming trips along with statistics on past travel. To do any real configuration, you have to go to the TripIt site where there are LOTS of options to configure your environment and share your information. TripIt also has a pro version that enables itinerary monitoring, travel alerts, alternate flights, and communication with an inner circle of your key people (like family or assistants) who "need to know."

Company BUZZ

Company BUZZ is actually a Twitter-powered application. It lets you see what others are saying about your company or about companies or keywords that you specify. It pulls its information from the Twitter world. To some degree, it is similar to Google Alerts or TweetDeck (a 3rd-party Twitter application.)

It also lets you filter the "Twitterverse" for keywords, called "topics," that you want to follow. This is sort of like wiretapping the Twitter conversations of everyone in the world. How about that for power? This application shows only on your LinkedIn homepage to monitor the conversations without showing any negatives that might pop up to your LinkedIn connections.

Box.Net

 The Box.Net application has many functions. First and foremost, it is a collaboration tool, especially outside of LinkedIn. Secondarily, it is a means to get your electronic material into the hands of your target audience. Box.Net is best suited to DOCUMENTS or PDFs. Presentations are better hosted by SlideShare or Google Presentations.

If you have a white paper, a brochure, or some other document that you want to get into the hands of your target audience, the Box.net application is the way to go. From your LinkedIn profile, people can easily click on the document and download it right from within LinkedIn. It is a great way to provide value to your network. When you provide that value easily and for free, people will remember.

Huddle Workspaces

 Huddle is an application that, like Box.net, is highly collaborative. The full-blown application is very powerful, and you can access much of that power directly from your LinkedIn profile. They provide 1GB of space in the free package. It also allows online editing of files, so you don't have to have the standard word processing or spreadsheet applications on the PC from which you are accessing your account.

WordPress

 WordPress is the world's #1 blogging platform. It has prime location in LinkedIn right near the top of the applications listing. You must already have a WordPress blog account and an active blog prior to adding it to your LinkedIn profile. The place to start the process is at **www.WordPress.com**. There are many great books available about WordPress, including *WordPress For Dummies*.

Don't have a WordPress blog? You can also add someone else's blog to your profile. All you need to know is the blog URL. Does your company have a blog? You can use it. There are reasons why you might use someone else's blog, and other reasons you would not. That is a discussion for another time. If you would like some help determining the strategy that is right for you, contact us at training@integratedalliances.com.

A little bit on WordPress itself:

There are two "flavors" of WordPress, and both can be free/low cost. The **WordPress.COM** site is fully hosted by WordPress and is very simple to use. The **WordPress.ORG** site offers the WordPress software free-of-charge to users who wish to host it on their own servers, or who wish to pay to have someone else host it for them.

What's the difference? The fully hosted **WordPress.COM** site does not provide for much customization you are rather "locked down" in your ability to customize the application. That is part of what makes it so simple. On the other hand, the **WordPress.ORG** site is extremely rich in customization and it has a wealth of 3rd-party tools and plug-ins (most of which are free) that can add incredible functionality to your website/blog environment. In fact, many people use their **WordPress.ORG** site as their main website. It is just that powerful. For a great example of this, visit **www.RockTheWorldBook.com**!

Blog Link

While WordPress is the #1 blogging platform, there are others that share the spotlight. TypePad by Google is one of the better alternatives. Blog Link supports all platforms "including TypePad, Movable Type, Vox, **Wordpress.com**, **Wordpress.org**, Blogger, LiveJournal, and many more. And it is Powered by TypePad technology."[1]

Blog Link ties your blog on any platform to your LinkedIn profile much like WordPress. It is a 3rd party application to BOTH LinkedIn AND to your blog by a company named Six Apart. With Blog Link, your blog postings appear directly inside your LinkedIn profile. The difference is that you have Linkedin, your blog, and Blog Link to work with rather than just LinkedIn and WordPress. The look and feel is different as well, with a less-obtrusive header. Try both, or look at other profiles to see which you prefer.

---

[1] http://www.linkedin.com *under the Blog Link application description.*

This is a fabulous application for bookclubbers! Somepeople are just avid readers. Whether or not you love to read, you can take advantage of this application. People like to see what you might recommend, what you feel is important. Recommending good books is one way you can provide value to your connections and a way to start conversations.

This application is one of the most popular on LinkedIn, partly because of its ease of use. It puts the pictures of two books directly on your profile and links off to a list of books that you wish to spotlight. Of course, there is a tie-in for people to click through to actually BUY these books and others off the Amazon.com website.

One strategy here is to put books in your profile that represent the industry in which you work or in which your customers and/or partners reside. Another strategy is more personal. In this case, you might list the non-work books that you are reading, have read, or want to read. Select books that represent your interests and who you are, giving people a chance to get to know you better without having to pick up the phone.

This is also a good way to create relationships with the authors. Send them a note and let them know that you are promoting their work. You will be surprised how appreciative many of them are. You can also follow the reading lists of other people in or outside of your network, making comments on the books they highlight. This is an interesting way to get conversations going with people with whom you wish to connect. You do not have to be a Tier 1 connection to follow the reading list of anyone.

LinkedIn Polls

This simple application, another application developed by LinkedIn, is actually very popular and very useful. It lets you create a bit of buzz around a topic and allows you to see some interesting results that you might not expect. It is rather limited in that it only lets you ask ONE question with a maximum of FIVE options, so it can't be used as a "survey."

When people come to your profile and answer the poll question, they can see the results of the poll. The poll can stay up as long as you like, although it is good housekeeping to change it every couple of months at the very least. You can also promote/share your poll question, much like you promote an event or send a message.

LinkedIn now allows every user to display their Twitter ID(s) in the header area of their LinkedIn profile. When you enable Tweets, it is also simple to see the Twitter updates of all of your followers and to tweet, reply, and re-tweet quickly. The interface is simple, providing a snapshot of the Tweets (Overview) of your followers, or of the Tweets (My Tweets) if your main Twitter account. From both of these tabs, you can update your Twitter status. If you include the #in or #li, your post will also update your LinkedIn status, although it is not instant.

From the application's Settings tab, you can quickly adjust which Twitter account should be displayed on your profile. The Twitter ID(s) associated with your LinkedIn profile are determined in the Settings area (see Chapter 8 for detailed instructions).

You will find detailed information about how to coordinate your status update on LinkedIn with your Twitter account(s) in Chapter 3 (Your Status) and in Chapter 8 (Account and Settings).

SAP Community BIO

SAP is a software tool used primarily by large businesses for very sophisticated CRM applications. It is akin to **SalesForce.com** in many ways, but intended for larger companies that often spend millions on its implementation. LinkedIn has an application that caters to SAP developers, analysts, consultants, and administrators, allowing them to promote their professional credentials, membership, and SAP community contributions on their LinkedIn profiles. Once the application is enabled, this information is fed directly from the user's SAP Community BIO.

Everyone wants to be a rock star!

No animals were harmed in the
making of this book.

Appendix A – The IA LinkedIn Profile Inventories

Here is the promised inventory blueprint for helping you get the most out of LinkedIn. It consists of ten steps that guide you through the "data collection" part of creating your profile. Use this in conjunction with the worksheet available online at www.RockTheWorldBook.com/Extras.

To get started, you will need your resume, any bio, as much information as you can find about current and previous companies and a word processing software or pen and paper. That's all!

Step 1 – Keyword Inventory

In its most fundamental element, there are two basic reasons people use LinkedIn – to find and to be found. In this book, we help you to prepare to be found. Focus on the fact that you are creating an attraction strategy from your headline, to your summary, to all the keywords that enable people to locate your profile so they can determine if they want to do business with you.

When people are looking for someone like you, they typically use the LinkedIn Search screen. In most cases, they search on one of more of the following criteria, listed in decreasing order of importance:

- Keywords

- Name

- Job titles

- Companies

Knowing this might cause you to think that a little extra attention to keywords is probably a good thing. You would be right! So let's go over some strategies.

Take a look at things from the perspective of the user who might try to find you. What words would they use to find you from among the millions of

LinkedIn users? Think in terms of their finding you for the purpose that you wish to be found.

Step 1 – Strategize: write down all the words and phrases you wish to be found under.

Does this sound like Search Engine Optimization (SEO) for a website? You bet! Some good ways to find new words are to ask your newest customers how they found you. What were they thinking of when they went looking for someone like you? You want to ask your new customers because they haven't learned your language yet. Also, if you have a Google AdWords account, what are the words that you use in it? Make sure those are in your Profile. What about your competitors? How are they found? What words or phrases are in their profile that fit you well? If they show up in search results, wouldn't you want to show up too? At least with them, if not ahead of them!

 Put these words one per line in Microsoft Word or Excel. Then use the thesaurus function to see what other words might fit. Add them to the list. These are the words that you want to weave throughout your profile.

 Once you have your list, show it to others who know you and that you trust. Ask them what you missed. Sort them by order of importance, using the ones at the top of this list most often, especially in your headline, titles, and specialties areas.

Step 2 – Employment and Job Title Inventory

Step Two is to take an inventory of all the paid and volunteer positions that you have held, ALL of them. There is no qualifying here; it is all about quantity, a brainstorming session. If you held multiple positions at the same company make note of all of them. Pay particular attention to job titles. You can probably get most of this from your resume. If you have/had a side business, note it as well.

At this point it is NOT relevant to note what you did at particular jobs. Is this starting to sound a little different than a resume? Well, it should! A resume is particularly big on what you did at each of these jobs. It might even have statistics. That is not important here yet.

Step 3 - Work Date Inventory

Step Three is to make note ABOUT when you were at these positions. You can probably get this from your resume as well. Don't worry about gaps or overlaps in the dates.

Step 4 - Goals Inventory

Decide for yourself, in brainstorm mode, what you may wish to accomplish in your career, in your life, on LinkedIn. This will help you when crafting your summary.

Examples:

I would like to change careers or industries, perhaps to...

I would like a more senior role

I would like to relocate to...

I want to do more public speaking

I want to find more security projects

People like to see what you are about going forward. Don't make them read between the lines. Spell it out, but be brief. Be sure to indicate why your previous experience lends itself to what you do now, and to what you want to do in the future.

Step 5 - Experience and Skills Inventory

This is an area that maps to the resume a bit, but you can take it to a new level with LinkedIn. Remember, LinkedIn is a "forward-looking" tool. Your experience and skills is especially important if it pertains to where you are headed, or if it helps explain how you got to where you are. This lends to your credibility. The information is a key part of your Summary and Specialties sections.

Examples of what may go in your Summary Section (typically sentences and phrases):

Developed and implemented merger strategy

Implemented Microsoft to Linux conversion

Converted in-house database to a web database

Oversaw expansion into new territories

Managed team of 12 sales professionals in three states

Worked in Eastern Europe for ten years

An example of what may go in your Specialties section - typically words or phrases separated by commas *(use common acronyms/abbreviations separated from the full description by a comma)*:

Microsoft Certified Systems Engineer, MSCE, Novell, Hewlett Packard, HP, Customer Relationship Manager Software, CRM, Siebel, Oracle

What NOT to include:

If it doesn't pertain to your future or if it is not an important credential, it can tend to cloud the picture and reduce the impact of the words that DO matter most. Consider leaving it out. If it is a statistic, leave it out unless it is especially relevant.

Step 6 – Education Inventory

What schooling have you had from high school on? Do a thorough inventory of all the places where you went to school, took classes, attended workshops, did online learning. This is a brainstorming session as well.

Part of this is to drive a feature of LinkedIn called Classmates, where LinkedIn matches you up with others who were at those institutions when you were. It can only match you up if it knows you were there and it will only know you were there if you include it.

Things to be sure to gather are:

- College – This is a no-brainer. List all of the colleges you attended if it was for AT LEAST one semester. Undergrad, post grad., etc.

- Trade Schools

- Specialty education including certification training, special classes to learn a specific skill (for example, Integrated Alliances University)

- High School

Do you have additional credentials or certifications? Note the full name and any abbreviations. For example a Microsoft Certified Systems Engineer is also a MSCE. A Mechanical Engineer is also an ME. You can list this in education to indicate where you received Certification and what "Degree" you earned. You can also list this under Honor and Awards as noted earlier.

Think long and hard to come up with a comprehensive list; people may search on these exact things and you want them to find you. You may choose not to use all of these, but this step is still important. It is easier to cut things out than to have to think of more to add in.

Step 7– Websites Inventory

LinkedIn allows you to list up to three websites on your profile. It lets you tie your profile to your business. Remember, we are in brainstorm mode here so don't be critical.

Do you have a company website?

Do you have a personal website; and is it professional or entirely personal?

Are you active in any associations or groups that have a Website?

Are you an affiliate of an online community or service provider?

Do you use any other social media platform where you would like to build a network?

Step 8 – Interests Inventory

Having common interests with someone can make a relationship much stronger. It is also a great starting point for a conversation that may lead to business or a referral. LinkedIn does a good job of making it easy to find people with similar interests. We have a lot of success stories from people who have made connections because of a common interest in music, muscle cars or favorite authors, which then brought about business opportunities because of the relationships that formed.

Make a list of the things you are currently genuinely interested in. This does not mean that you have to be active in them, just interested in them. Use broad terms and then drill down as well (e.g. football, college football, Arizona State, Sun Devils, music, rock and roll, Pink Floyd, Maroon 5, U2, international travel).

Here are some ideas:

- Sports – golf, tennis, working out, exercise, weight lifting, car racing, drag racing, swimming, mountain biking

- Hobbies – woodworking, traveling, model airplanes, remodeling, baseball cards

- Others – parenting, coaching, genealogy, reading

Step 9 – Associations and Group Involvement Inventory

LinkedIn does a really good job of tracking associations and groups and has some really great tools for finding others that share these common bonds with you. Still in brainstorm mode, think of the associations and groups you can say you are affiliated with in one way or another. You do not have to be a current member; you do not have to be tightly associated either.

These questions might help you:

- Are you part of any professional association? Note full names and acronyms or abbreviations.

- Do you attend any association functions regularly?

- Look in the past and ask the same questions?

- What associations do your customers or vendors belong to that might correlate to your work?

Some examples might include:

- Colorado Athletic Club, CAC

- Alpha Tau Omega Fraternity, ATO

- Denver Telecom Professionals, DTP

- Network Denver

- Integrated Alliances

- Denver Metro Chamber of Commerce, DMCC

- Little League Baseball coach (or Little League baseball parent)

- Chess Club

- American Automobile Association, AAA

- Places where you volunteer

Step 10 – Honors and Awards Inventory

Were you ever recognized for anything that is noteworthy? How about any of these:

- Presidents Club

- Honor Student

- Dean's List

- Salesman of the month

- Voted most likely to succeed

That gives us some good stuff to work with, doesn't it? Llook at what inventories map to which fields on your LinkedIn profile. Throughout the book, we suggested some best practices that come from years of experience helping people on LinkedIn, in career development, and in helping professionals strengthen their online reputations.

Appendix B – LinkedIn Groups

Musical interests are well-represented in LinkedIn Groups. A quick LinkedIn Groups search on the keyword "Music" yields over 1,500 Groups, and "Band" yields another 300. There are four LinkedIn Groups about the Grateful Dead and three that focus on, or at least mention Led Zeppelin in their description. While this is not the reason that we cover LinkedIn Groups in this book, it is a nice coincidence. I was at a recent Dead show (no longer the Grateful Dead) and there were lots of people with grey hair "tweeting" all around. Some of them even drove a Cadillac; like me!

One of the most powerful features of LinkedIn is LinkedIn Groups. It has been around for a long time actually, but in 2008 it really started picking up steam and there are now hundreds of thousands of LinkedIn Groups.

Groups are tightly tied to LinkedIn profiles so we will cover it here. As a user, you can join up to 50 Groups and that should be plenty. We suggest that you identify 30 or so groups to join for starters and we will show you how to identify and join them.

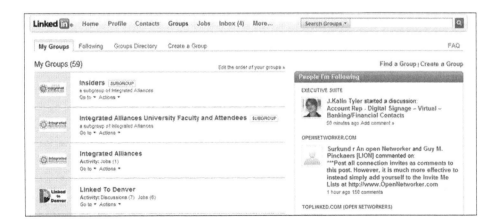

You might actually find LinkedIn Groups so interesting that you want to start your own LinkedIn Group. That is a topic for my upcoming book focused on LinkedIn Groups. It follows the Integrated Alliances methodology for being successful operating YOUR OWN LinkedIn Group. Another option is to attend an Integrated Alliances LinkedIn Groups training class, which is delivered regularly via webinar in our live workshops coast to coast or available on demand. Find information at **www.IASocialMedia.com/Training.**

From a 10,000-foot view, what are LinkedIn Groups?

LinkedIn Groups are really a large number of independent gathering places on the LinkedIn site for people to come together over a topic that might be:

1. A professional interest like Search Engine Optimization

2. A professional association like the Business Marketing Association

3. A region like Denver or Colorado

4. A hobby like Corvettes or Horses

5. A sport like Basketball or Tennis

6. A fan club like Led Zeppelin or The Grateful Dead

7. A cause like At Risk Children or Breast Cancer

8. An alma mater like Arizona State University (mine)

Step 1 – DETERMINE YOUR GOALS for LinkedIn Groups

It will be different for everyone to a great degree. Here are some popular and noble goals:

1. To learn new ideas, best practices, event happenings and more from others in your line of business or in your region.

2. To meet others in your line of business, at your professional level or in your region.

3. To pose questions to an audience that can help you.

4. To get a nifty logo to post on your Profile.

Step 2 - DEVELOP A STRATEGY for identifying which LinkedIn Groups to join

Here is one to consider as a starting point. Pick at least three groups to join in each of these categories:

1. Groups in your profession

2. Groups in your region (usually city or state)

3. Groups of personal interest (hobby)

4. Groups that might contain prospects or customers

5. Groups that might contain possible business partners

6. Any alma mater that might have a group

 The invitation process benefits tremendously from your membership in LinkedIn Groups. When inviting another individual to join your LinkedIn network, one of the options presented is Groups & Associations (along with Colleagues, Classmates, etc.) By selecting this option, and choosing one of the LinkedIn Groups that you share, the other individuals may be more likely to accept your invitation and may even take a closer look at doing business with you. After all, you have identified a mutual interest.

Think about getting an invitation, perhaps from someone you do not know, that references a LinkedIn Group that you respect, one that is in your industry or simply one that looks and sounds good to you. Doesn't it make you more interested in that person?

Step 3 - FIND the groups that will help you accomplish your goals

There are two primary methods to find LinkedIn Groups. The first is by means of the Group Search function and the second is by clicking directly on the icon of LinkedIn Groups that you see on other people's profiles.

The Group search function makes it very easy to find groups of interest to you based on KEYWORDS. You can access LinkedIn Groups area from ANY page on LinkedIn. It is always on the navigation bar. Simply click on the word "Groups" and you will go to the main page for LinkedIn Groups where the groups you belong to are listed. To the right is the Find a Group field. Also, a sub-menu of the Groups tab is Groups Directory, which highlights featured groups and provides a "Search Groups" interface.

If you are familiar with the Keyword search function on LinkedIn (People button or Companies button) then this will be old hat for you. If not, we will provide a little search education for you here.

Long ago, in the time of Abraham Lincoln, a brilliant mathematician named George Boole created a mathematical methodology that is used in junior high classrooms to this day. It is based around the principle of "sets."

Let's try and compress an entire math class into a few lines of text. Roll up your sleeves!

If an object is big AND it is red then it is a member of the "BIG AND RED" set. It must be BOTH big and red.

If that object is big OR it is red, then it is a member of the "BIG OR RED" set. It need not be BOTH, just one or the other.

This principle is further enhanced by some other basic algebra, such as using brackets like ( ).

For example the object might be big and (red or blue.)

I hope you get the idea. Because next, we add the concept of phrases and it gets more definitive. Quotation marks (aka "") are used here. An example tells the story best.

"dark blue" OR blue

Here are some complex examples:

("dark blue" OR blue OR red) AND big

Translate that, in this case, to the LinkedIn Groups search and it like this:

Colorado AND Marketing

or

(Denver or Colorado) and Marketing

or

("search engine optimization" OR SEO) AND (Colorado OR Denver)

Now that we have real examples, let's translate this into actually finding LinkedIn groups. Use this process to get going:

1. From any page, hover over Groups on the navigation menu and select Groups Directory, or click on the word Groups on the left navigation bar then click on the Find a Group link on the right.

2. In the Search Groups keyword field on the left, enter the phrase that you might like to search. Do not pay any attention to the categories and languages options for now.

The results appear in descending order of largest to smallest membership size. They also display the Group Summary and logo.

Step 4- JOIN Groups from the Group Search Screen

When searching in the Group Search, this step is actually very easy. The "Join this group" text link appears in each search listing. You are one click away from REQUESTING to join the group.

Some groups will automatically approve you and others will require the group manager to make a "judgment." If you are not approved or if it seems to take a long time to get approved (two to three weeks or more,) send a message to the group manager, or withdraw the request and find another.

Here are some hot tips that come from my upcoming book dedicated specifically to LinkedIn Groups. They are also included in the Integrated Alliances LinkedIn Groups training.

Tip! *Only join the top groups. Search results are listed in order of largest to smallest. If there are less than 500 members, think twice, unless there is a specific reason that the group interests you. Join the top two or three from each of the categories listed earlier.*

Tip! *The group manager is listed when you request to join. Click on the link and invite the group manager to connect to you. Write a nice custom note. These are typically well-connected people so it is usually beneficial to connect with them as well.*

Tip! *Order the LinkedIn groups in a way that makes the most sense to you personally. Put the most strategic groups based on how frequently you will access it at the top. You can get to this from the Account and Settings section. The Settings link appears at the top on every LinkedIn page. It is found in the lower left corner of the Settings options. It is fairly obvious what to do if you spend just a few minutes there.*

Step 5 - FIND AND JOIN LinkedIn Groups from other LinkedIn Profiles

During the course of your routine use of LinkedIn, you are going to look at lots of profiles. Most of these individuals will now be members of at least SOME LinkedIn Groups. LinkedIn makes it incredibly easy for you to join groups when you see that others are members too.

If you keyword search using the People button or the LinkedIn Advanced Search screen, you will find lots of interesting people that already belong to LinkedIn Groups. Perhaps groups that would also be of interest to YOU? Here are some ideas for individuals that you might want to locate:

1. People in the same profession as you. They deal with many of the same issues meaning that there is insider knowledge that can be shared.

2. People, at your same level in the "org chart." C-levels might seek out other C-levels, or directors other directors, for example.

3. People that might constitute customers or business partners. This is where they are, and now you can mix and mingle with them where they spend their time – in LinkedIn Groups.

Simply click on the logo's you see at the bottom of a user's profiles. This will take you directly to the Join Group screen for that particular LinkedIn Group. So long as you are not already enrolled in 50 groups, you can request to join on the spot. It's just that easy.

Step 6 – Look into joining LinkedIn SUBGROUPS

LinkedIn now has an interesting feature called Subgroups. Once you are a member of a LinkedIn Group, you can take it to the next level IN SOME GROUPS - those that have taken the plunge and established subgroups to their main group. As this feature is adopted more and more by group managers, there will be increased time spent within these subgroups. The idea of a subgroup is much like a breakout session at a conference. A subgroup is also analogous to Special Interest Group within what might already be a Special Interest Group.

The larger and broader groups are more likely to have subgroups in place. You can take a look at the Linked To Denver Group (www.LinkToDenver.com) to see subgroups in action. There should be lots of LinkedIn subgroups by the time you read this.

You can join up to 50 subgroups and they DO NOT count against Linke-dIn's limit of 50 main groups that a user may join. To some extent, that is like joining 100 LinkedIn groups, although subgroups will have a much smaller, tighter audience.

Appendix C – How Far Can You Take It?

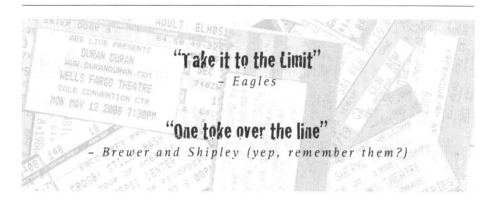

"Take it to the Limit"
– Eagles

"One toke over the line"
– Brewer and Shipley (yep, remember them?)

With but a few exceptions, everything in LinkedIn has its limits. We thought it might be a good exercise to put the Profile limits all in one place.

We suggest that, in terms of characters used, you should "take it to the limit" where we indicate below. Fortunately, LinkedIn will, in most cases, tell you when you are "one toke over the line" and tell you just how many characters you are over the limit. It is even in nice red text so you really can't miss it.

For example, if you paste text into your summary text box, click on "Save" and get an error message, it will tell you that have used 2,050 characters and you are only allowed 2,000. It won't let you save it until you comply with the limits. The following numbers indicate the maximum number of characters allowed in each field type.

Number of Profiles you can have – legally one, technically there is no limit

Picture: 4 MB file upload that results in an 80 x 80 pixel picture

First Name – 20
Last Name – 40

Former/Maiden Name – 40

Headline – 120
Website Custom Tag – 31
Status field – 140
Public Profile URL – 46

Summary – 2,000
Specialties – 500

Number of Companies – unlimited
Company Name - 100
Position (Job) Title – 100
Position Description – 2,000

Number of Educational Institutions - unlimited
Education/Degree – 100
Education/Fields of study – 100
Education/Activities and Societies – 500
Education/Additional Notes – 1,000

Number of recommendations – unlimited
Number of characters in a recommendation
        – more than you should ever use!

Interests – 1,000
Groups and Associations – 1,000
Honors and Awards – 1,000
Contact Settings – 1,000+ (if you go over in this field, it simply will not
        save your changes. The most we have seen is 1,495 characters, but
        the total is less than 2,000.)

Appendix D – Some Important Definitions – the Glossary

"Stand for something" (or you'll fall for anything)
– John Mellencamp

It is easy to throw words around and think that everyone knows what you mean. What does "contact" stand for? How about "connection" or other words? When you define the terms, you get everyone on the same page. You always know where John Mellencamp stands on things. He is the very definition of Rock & Roll - no filler, no substitute, nothing artificial. He is rock in its purest, most definitive sense.

Connection

Someone with whom you are directly connected on LinkedIn. Sometimes you will see the word Direct or Tier 1 used or maybe someone may be described as being a "1." These phrases all mean the same thing. You have special capabilities with your Tier 1 connections. Beside the name of each person who is a peer, you will see "1st" beside their name indicating their relationship to you. Their first level connections, with whom you are not connected, will display "2nd", and the connections of your Tier 2 connections will display "3rd". Finally, LinkedIn indicates people with whom you share a group as "Group". These are treated in sort results the same as Tier 2s.

Contact

Someone whose contact information has been imported into your LinkedIn space, but is not yet connected to you (these are like prospects.)

InMail

An inner-platform email message that is sent through the system usually to second or third level connections. It replaces the Introduction process. It is NOT used or needed between direct Tier 1 connections. A certain number of InMails are granted monthly to paid subscribers based on their level of service.

Introduction

A request for a message along with your contact information passed through one individual to another for a business introduction. There are two levels of introduction, through one person to get to a 2nd level connection, or through two to get to a 3rd level connection. This is sort of like passing notes in class ... not a recommendation or endorsement. It is best not to use this for Tier 3 connections as the introduction can often be delayed, causing you to run out of available introductions.

Invitation

Asking someone to "join your professional network on LinkedIn." The end result is that each becomes a part of the other's network of LinkedIn contacts, giving both the ability to search through more records to find opportunities. It doesn't matter who invites whom, the result is being connected just as if one person picked up the phone to call the other and got an answer.

Network

The people to whom you are directly connected on LinkedIn, their direct connections and their direct connections – three levels deep. It also includes people with whom you share a group – these are treated as Tier 2 connections when sorting search results by "Relationship."

OpenLink

These messages are when a paid subscriber indicates their willingness to accept InMail from anyone. User send OpenLink members a free InMail. When paid subscribers send an OpenLink message, it is not counted against their available InMails.

Profile

Your personal identity on LinkedIn. It is the equivalent of a professional Web page about you with special links and other features that allow you to impact your business.

Search

Looking for people, companies, or groups on LinkedIn based on specific information. It may be a name, a location, a keyword, or other search criteria. Combining the power of the search three levels deep and reach into Group relationships with many options to find specific or targeted results. This is the most powerful feature of LinkedIn. A really well built-out and SEO-friendly profile will make your LinkedIn Profile more searchable and, therefore, more findable. (By the way, SEO stands for Search Engine Optimized.)

Search Engine Optimization (SEO)

Computer programs ("bots") constantly look through the Internet, LinkedIn and other platforms to find information based on a user's search criteria. It is based on both words and/or phrases. In the LinkedIn world, people can find your LinkedIn Profile through its internal search function. Better yet, LinkedIn Profiles are fully indexed – searchable – by Google and most other search engines as well, making your presence on LinkedIn, and a well-built profile, even more important.

Tier

A tier indicates relationship level. It defines how many people are between you and someone else in terms of relationships. Another way to think of this is that a Tier 1 connection is directly connected to you; a Tier 2 connection is someone connected to them. There are three Tiers in LinkedIn. Group members are like friends with whom you share a common interest.

The Grammy Goes To ...

In promoting the book, we had a lot of ideas thrown at us. It brought me back to a time where sample products and free music were part of the job. In this case we had access to a lot of Web 2.0 tools that allowed us to make this whole process fun, engaging, and quick.

Central to our initiative was a program called **CrowdCampaign.com.** Our new friends over there, Clinton Bonner and Mike Buckbee, engineered a hosted scoring application. They sought a hard-hitting audience of people just like those that we surround ourselves with – and they like Rock & Roll!

The contest officially lasted ten days, although a dozen or so were allowed to be part of a pre-trial test. Every few days software enhancements were made to add functionality and increase usability. We became a virtual team on this project.

The contest was based on a combination of votes received, profile completeness, network size and "style points." For a complete description of the contest and links to the winners' profiles, check out **www.rocktheworldbook.com/contest**

Top Vote Getter - also highest raw score!

Jeff Hodgkinson

Headline: Sr. Program Manager @ Intel Corp | Program & Project Mgmt Coach | PMI SME

LinkedIn URL: www.LinkedIn.com/in/jeffhodgkinson

Twitter ID: @JGHMESA

Top Dual Language Profile - She rocks our world!

Jeanet Bathoorn

Headline: Linkedin Workshops | Trainer Online Netwerken | Linkedin & Twitter Expert | Social Networker | Spreker

LinkedIn URL: www.linkedin.com/in/jeanetbathoorn

Twitter ID: @jeanetbathoorn

Mark Amtower

Headline: Mentor to current & future Government Market Masters

LinkedIn URL: www.linkedin.com/in/markamtower

Twitter ID: @amtower

Patrick O'Malley

Headline: Social media Training, Keynote Speaking, Consulting, see videos @ www.PatrickOmalley.com

LinkedIn URL: www.linkedin.com/in/patrickomalley

Twitter ID: @617patrick

J.D. Gershbein

Headline: OWLISH COMMUNICATIONS   LINKEDIN Profile Writer   LINKEDIN Trainer   LINKEDIN Speaker   BUSINESS CARTOONIST

LinkedIn URL: www.linkedin.com/in/jdgershbein

LinkedIn URL: JDGershbein

Wendy Brache

Headline: Senior Online Marketing Consultant | Online Presence Specialist | Sales Force Branding | High Tech B2B | Social media

LinkedIn URL: www.linkedin.com/in/wendybrache

Twitter ID: @wendybrache

Liz Isaacs

Headline: Work Smart. Be Heard. Be Remembered. Passionate Writing & Marketing Communications Strategist | Author | Screenwriter

LinkedIn URL: www.linkedin.com/in/lotuswritingcommunications

Twitter ID: @lizisaacslwc

Spencer Maus

> **Headline:** Senior Executive - Media, Public & Investor Relations, Communications, Social media Strategist/Tactician
>
> **LinkedIn URL:** www.linkedin.com/in/spencermaus
>
> **Twitter ID:** @spencerconnect

Other Finalists (high scorers)

Mark Williams (United Kingdom)

Octavio Ballesta (Venezuela)

Flyn Penoyer (San Francisco, CA)

Peter Pittman (Denver, CO)

Peter Brissette (Denver, CO)

Lesley Dewar (Perth, Australia)

Honorable Mentions

Steve Patrizi – Best submission by a LinkedIn Corp. employee

Don Cooper – For great formatting and use of Summary and Specialties

Heather Krasna – For excellent example of maiden name field

Bryan C. Webb – "Common misspellings of my name" - well done!

Jose Eduardo Motta Garcia – For fun LinkedIn Group memberships including Pink Floyd and Pearl Jam

The Judges

Mike O'Neil	www.linkedin.com/in/mikeoneil
Lori Ruff	www.linkedin.com/in/loriruff
Dave Taylor	www.linkedin.com/in/davetaylor
Melissa Giovagnoli	www.linkedin.com/in/networlding

A note about the Publisher and Charitable giving

I want to share a special point regarding our publisher, Networlding, and Melissa Giovagnoli, founder and CEO. I came to Melissa a couple of months ago when I was trying to figure out my options regarding publishing. Melissa, having published 11 books and skilled in helping authors get published and on the charts, she offered to take on the role of publisher for my book.

I jumped at the opportunity and would have been happy to pay for her services. But, Melissa insisted that the only compensation she wanted was to have me take 10% of the book's net profits and donate them to, as she put it, "initiatives that help young professionals get 'smart starts' in their careers."

Well, of course, I took her up on her offer. And ever since, I have experienced a wonderful collaboration with her team – a group comprised of top practitioners in publishing. So, thank you, Melissa. I look forward to honoring your request to "pay it forward" with 10% of this book's net proceeds going to benefit the Rock the World 2029 Initiative a non-profit effort to enable young entrepreneurs to obtain professional business coaching.

This book is about giving out (giving away) four years of hard-earned LinkedIn training and consulting expertise. The entire social media industry is about giving thereby getting more back, all as a result of NOT tying the inputs directly to the outputs. It's the concept of Karma in practice. This book benefits young entrepreneurs by giving them access to a great band manager in the form of professional business coaching they might never get otherwise.

The LinkedIn Relationship

We must be very clear in stating that Integrated Alliances is not associated with LinkedIn in any way. We are constantly asked this question as we provide so much support to the LinkedIn end-user community, and have done so for many years. It is simply not the case.

The same statement goes for Twitter, Facebook and all of the other social media platforms. IA operates in a manner much like a "for profit" association, a user group, or a fan club that anticipates the needs of the LinkedIn and social media user community and we respond to serve those needs.

That said we wish to thank LinkedIn for many things:

- First, for creating this incredible platform, which is so refined to be representative of the needs of professionals in an online networking community. Because of the power and influence of LinkedIn, today this industry has a strong business focus. In fact, IA might simply be another business networking association like many others. Many thousands of people have their jobs today because of LinkedIn's foresight, and I don't just mean jobs at LinkedIn. An entire industry has sprung up in which IA has played a major role. This industry employs thousands, perhaps tens of thousands, of business professionals who would have never pictured themselves in such an exciting role or working for such an interesting company as they do now.

- Second, for their sponsorship of the early Integrated Alliances LinkedIn Hands-on Workshops way back in Q1 2006. LinkedIn was generous to help us launch the LinkedIn training programs from the ground level with some financial backing.

- Third, for their continued product development and enhancements that provide business users with increased functionality, which allow companies to find customers, partners, and employees, and enable displaced individuals to find needed employment. The lives of most users are better as a result.

Special thanks go directly to **Reid Hoffman** for the help he provided to IA's strategic business partner, The Rockies Venture Club by keynoting the RVC Colorado Capital Conference back in June 2006. His appearance helped cement LinkedIn as the quintessential online business capital player in Colorado that it is today. As a result of Reid's appearance and influence, IA has received a significant amount of LinkedIn training and consulting business opportunities that continue 4 years later.

Thanks LinkedIn!

Author Mike O'Neil with LinkedIn Executive Chairman and Co-Founder Reid Hoffman at Colorado Capital Conference, 2006

Rock is Timeless

Rock & Roll is timeless. This book has been designed to be timeless as well. Although no technology-related book in this day and age can keep from getting obsolete nearly the day it is printed, we have taken steps to stay ahead of the curve of current technology. Unlike a car losing its value the moment you drive it off the showroom floor, you don't have to worry about your investment here losing value.

Rock the World with your Online Presence has an snazzy online component to keep you up to date, to provide collaboration, and to allow us to stay engaged with one another. After all, social media is first about relationships, and our relationship with you is important to us.

Our online site ensures that you have the latest information, tips, and tricks to keep your profile at multi-platinum status. It continues the Rock & Roll attitude of the book and even takes it to a whole new dimension.

Visit anytime for timely information: www.rocktheworldbook.com/extras

The artist born as Mike O'Neil

Author, Mike O'Neil is the founder of Integrated Alliances (IA) and IA Social Media. To say IA really knows social media would be a bit of an understatement. The company is well endowed with experts, associates, and fans who are generous and eager to share. IA team members are pioneer users, and trainers who have long led the social media charge for business.

Since 2003, IA has led the Business-to-Business (B2B) networking community in Colorado, hosting hundreds of networking events under the Social-Net and LinkedIn Live brands. When IA launched LinkedIn Training in early 2006, there were no LinkedIn trainings of ANY kind available. In fact people laughed – "What, you're going to train someone to use a Website? How hard can that be?"

We approached LinkedIn with the idea of a relationship, and even THEY did not see the need for training. They financed our first sessions; then sent us on our way to train and wished us "the best of luck".

Now, over 400 sessions later, IA has the most complete LinkedIn-oriented social media training and consulting offerings available anywhere. No longer "just" LinkedIn, the field includes all the popular areas of social media including Facebook, Twitter, YouTube, Wordpress and a host of others.
(For a complete listing of the 300+ social media sites available, check out www.wikipedia.com!)

While it's the suite of platforms that really matters the most for our clients (call it vegetable soup if you will), one must master the fine inner workings of the most important sites to gain a critical business advantage. That means LinkedIn, and LinkedIn profiles in particular, are the place to start. That need is what drives this book.

How does this apply for companies, teams and groups? Most of the concepts discussed in this book carry over to a company-driven, centralized approach. Indeed this is where IA does most of its professional services work. The issues are different much like a band has different issues from a solo singer/songwriter/guitarist.

IA provides advanced Social Media Services for individuals, companies, teams, groups and associations, so users can ENJOY and BENEFIT from social media NOW.

In this book, we have taken our long history of training and consulting and combined it with the knowledge of our most experienced and sought-after team members. We focus exclusively on making your LinkedIn profile the best it can be.

and the rest of the band...

Look at IA's in-person workshops and online training to see when and where we offer training. We have trained over 50 LinkedIn trainers all over the world and in 2009 began its IA Certified Trainer program. As such we have a growing presence and growing influence all over the world. We are always adjusting to keep up with this quickly evolving industry, so check our site often for the latest updates and resources.

Better yet, let IA do the heavy lifting for you and work with you to create your professional online presence. Once built, we will show you how to use it to your best advantage. That's a lot more enjoyable and significantly more effective use of your precious time than building it yourself.

Got a conference, convention, or gathering coming up? JAZZ IT UP by bringing The LinkedIn Rock Stars to speak or train for you. The vision and creative energies come from me, Mike O'Neil and Lori Ruff. On stage together, we have great energy and are often compared to Burns and Allen or Sonny and Cher.

If you are interested in any of our programs or services, connect with us on the web (www.IASocialMedia.com), via email (Training@IASocialMedia.com), or by phone (303-683-9600).

The Concert Experience

This book is not all-inclusive of LinkedIn. It is entirely focused on one aspect of your LinkedIn experience – how you, as an individual, look and present yourself to the outside business world.

There is a lot more to it than what we cover in these pages. It is part of a bigger picture, a larger process. This 1-2-3-4-5 process, stemming from years of experience, development and practical application maximizes your results and helps you look like a rock star on LinkedIn.

The book you are holding now is Step One in the IA methodology for LinkedIn. We recommend that you go through these steps in order, moving to the next when you feel you are well along.

The IA Methodology is this:

1   CRAFT A GREAT PROFILE that attracts others and represents you well.

2   BUILD YOUR NETWORK appropriately to make your profile visible to millions of others giving you a broad base of resources.

3   SEARCH and enjoy a large number of meaningful results.

4   REACH OUT and communicate with your peers, customers, vendors, business partners, fellow enthusiasts.

5   GET DOWN TO BUSINESS: create opportunities for you and your company.

Are there others at your company using LinkedIn? Are they peers, co-workers, team members, departments, divisions, or groups? There are unique opportunities as well as pitfalls when you begin to look at LinkedIn operations and LinkedIn profiles for teams or groups.

A search for your products or services should find each of these individuals. Yes, that is basic keyword searching. Your company or team or group should be represented by each individual in a consistent manner. Each individual associated with a company or group or team should look like they work together rather than not.

Do you want your employees to be responsible for writing and managing the corporate message? This book teaches you how to create your own image very well. It even helps you with a company portrayal to a degree. It is no substitute however, for a corporate marketing effort to develop an optimized, even official, text template to describe the organization.

Corporate LinkedIn Profile Templates and Company LinkedIn Profiles: There are additional strategies for using our methodology and strategies to build out your online presence in a team or company-wide environment. That is not only a service we provide for companies, teams and groups, but it is our next writing effort. Look for it soon at **www.RockTheWorldBook.com**.

Interested in group sales, a private concert, or sharing your thoughts? Reach us at **Promotions@RocktheWorldBook.com** *to purchase volume lots of the book, to have Mike and/or Lori speak, train, or provide consulting for you, or to send us your valuable feedback.*

Rock the World with your Online Presence: Song References

1. "The new frontier", Donald Fagan of Steely Dan, 1982, p14
2. "Deeper understanding", Kate Bush, 1989, p14
3. "Blue, blue sky", Alan Parsons Project, 1996, p15
4. "It's the end of the world as we know it", REM, 1987, p16
5. "The long run", The Eagles, 1979, p16
6. "No lookin' back", Michael McDonald, 1985, p16
7. "Start me up", The Rolling Stones, 1981, p20
8. "Show me the way", Peter Frampton, 1975, p22
9. "Helter skelter", The Beatles, 1968, p22
10. "Wanna' be startin' something", Michael Jackson, 1982, p27
11. "My hometown", Bruce Springsteen, 1985, p29
12. "Got to get you into my life", The Beatles, 1966, p30
13. "If you don't know me by now", Simply Red, 1989, p34
14. "Who are you?", The Who, 1978, p36
15. "Every day I write the book", Elvis Costello, 1983, p40
16. "What's your name?", Lynyrd Skynyrd, 1977, p44
17. "Who can it be now?", Men at Work, 1981, p47
18. "Shout it out loud", KISS, 1976, p49
19. "Kodachrome", Paul Simon, 1973, p52
20. "Photograph", Def Leppard, 1983, p52
21. "What's goin' on", Marvin Gaye, 1971, p55
22. "See me, feel me", The Who, 1970, p58
23. "Invisible touch", Genesis, 1986, p58
24. "Don't stop thinking about tomorrow", Fleetwood Mac, 1977, p62
25. "Livin' in the past", Jethro Tull, 1972, p62
26. "What you need", INXS, 1985, p62
27. "We've only just begun", Carpenters, 1970, p66
28. "Old Days", Chicago, 1975, p72
29. "Are you experienced?", Jimi Hendrix, 1967, p72
30. "School's out", Alice Cooper, 1972, p76
31. "My Old School", Steely Dan, 1973, p76

32. "I get by with a little help from my friends", The Beatles, 1967, p79
33. "You've got a friend", James Taylor, 1971, p79
34. "Like to get to know you well", Howard Jones, 1984, p88
35. "Two out of three ain't bad", Meat Loaf, 1977, p89
36. "The real me", The Who, 1973, p91
37. "True colors", Cyndi Lauper, 1986, p91
38. "A matter of trust", Billy Joel, 1986, p93
39. "Fame", David Bowie, 1975, p95
40. "Special", Garbage, 1998, p95
41. "Call me", Blondie, 1980, p97
42. "I can't go for that", Hall and Oates, 1981, p99
43. "Stayin' alive", The Bee Gees, 1977, p99
44. "Man in the mirror", Michael Jackson, 1988, p104
45. "Heard it through the grapevine", Marvin Gaye, 1968, p106
46. "Welcome to the machine", Pink Floyd, 1975, p110
47. "Message in a bottle", The Police, 1979, p116
48. "Don't you want me baby?", Human League, 1981, p116
49. "Walk this way", Aerosmith, 1975, p121
50. "All I want to do", Sheryl Crow, 1994, p121
51. "Run with the pack", Bad Company, 1976, p123
52. "We belong", Pat Benatar, 1984, p124
53. "Nobody's fault but mine", Led Zeppelin, 1976, p124
54. "Rikki, don't lose that number", Steely Dan, 1974, p126
55. "Every rose has its thorn", Poison, 1988, p132
56. "You ain't seen nothing yet", Bachman Turner Overdrive, 1974, p138
57. "Take it to the limit", The Eagles, 1975, p164
58. "One toke over the line", Brewer and Shipley, 1970, p164
59. "You've got to stand for something", John Mellencamp, 1985, p166
60. "What I got I wanna' give away", Luce, 2002, p172
61. "Takin' care of business", Bachman Turner Overdrive, 1973, p182

About the Authors

"Takin' care of business"

Bachman Turner Overdrive

This book is about how to strategically apply LinkedIn to BUSINESS and to YOU, the business person. The word "Social" in social media actually applies very little when it comes to LinkedIn. Many of the concepts presented in this book are equally applicable to the more-social platforms like Facebook. But make no bones about it, this is all about business! Isn't music a business? Yep – and a big one at that!

Mike O'Neil is an entrepreneur, an expert LinkedIn trainer and a former IT professional and sales engineer. In 2003, Mike founded Integrated Alliances (IA) as a professional business networking organization presenting business networking events, first in Colorado and now nationwide for providing the most effective business development gatherings for professionals who want to uncover business opportunities.

Mike expanded the role of Integrated Alliances in early 2006 as online networking gained in popularity. IA began training business professionals to use LinkedIn focused on business applications, and now IA has trained thousands of people in hundreds of sessions, including hands-on workshops and conferences across North America and in online webinars with a world-wide reach.

Mike became a LinkedIn user in January 2004 – user number 125,841.

Headquartered in Denver, CO, Mike has assembled a team of social media professionals represented in metropolitan areas coast to coast. Most of them he met or reconnected with through LinkedIn and other social media platforms. They typically have reached out to Mike to join his team of dynamic social media trainers and coaches and to become associated with the brand that is IA. In addition, IA has courted collaborative partnerships with some of the biggest names in this exploding industry.

After being introduced to Mike through LinkedIn, Lori Ruff joined the national expansion team in Charlotte, NC mid-2008. Later that year, she was asked to join the IA executive team, and did so with fervor. While I provide much of the vision, Lori is remarkable at making sure the right ideas are implemented at the right time. It is truly a brilliant partnership.

Her current career began in July 1996 when she founded a training and consulting firm winning government contracts, corporate clients, and multiple awards. Ruff joined the LinkedIn community in July 2005 when Facebook was still in school. She has long been known as a connector of people and now uses social networking to enhance those skills. She has become a respected authority in the world of Social Media and LinkedIn training. According to Toplinked.com, Lori is one of the top ten most connected women on LinkedIn.

Today Lori is a popular speaker, trainer and online business reputation consultant delivering with poise and high energy. She has presented over 1,800 hours representing almost 800 training sessions and seminar appearances to audiences as large as 500. She is also a Microsoft Certified Master Instructor and delivers on topics such as customer service, leadership, visioning, personal development, and career transition.

Mike and Lori in Concert T's –
Mike prefers Pink Floyd while
fellow IA partner Lori Ruff prefers
REO Speedwagon

Mike's Concert TIXS–
Sorting through 500+ ticket
stubs for the book